THE FASCIST PARTY IN WALES?

T0083752

The Fascist Party in Wales?

Plaid Cymru, Welsh Nationalism
and the Accusation of Fascism

Richard Wyn Jones

Translation by Richard Wyn Jones and Dafydd Jones

University of Wales Press
Cardiff
2014

www.uwp.co.uk

British Library Cataloguing-in-Publication Data.
A catalogue record for this book is available from the British Library.

ISBN   978-1-7831-6056-3
e-ISBN   978-1-7831-6057-0

This book was first published in Welsh in 2013 by the University of Wales Press as *'Y Blaid Ffasgaidd yng Nghymru': Plaid Cymru a'r Cyhuddiad o Ffasgaeth* (ISBN 978-0-7083-2650-3; e-ISBN 978-0-7083-2656-5), in the series Safbwyntiau: Gwleidyddiaeth Diwylliant Cymdeithas.

The University of Wales Press acknowledges the financial support of the Welsh Books Council.

Typeset in Wales by Eira Fenn Gaunt, Cardiff.
Printed by CPI Antony Rowe, Chippenham, Wiltshire

i Eli Stamnes,
un a wyddai o'r cychwyn cyntaf
mai pobl ryfedd ar y naw ydym ni'r Cymry. . .

CONTENTS

Preface

To celebrate the signing of the now infamous Munich Agreement on 30 September 1938, the then Lord Mayor of Cardiff, Alderman O. Cuthbert Purnell, ordered that the flags of the four states represented at the negotiations in the Bavarian capital be flown above City Hall. So it was that the flags of the United Kingdom, France, Italy and Germany were raised over the city. A Czechoslovak flag could not be located or it, too, would apparently have been flown alongside them to celebrate that country's forced dismemberment in the cause of 'peace in our time'. The provocation of seeing the swastika – since September 1935, also the German national flag – fly above the city proved too much for two outraged Labour members of the council, Alderman C. H. McCale and Councillor John Heginbottom, who duly hauled it down. At a subsequent, heated meeting of the council, their actions were vigorously defended by a number of their party colleagues. One of these, A. J. Williams, protested that it would 'surely have been better to raise the Russian flag, because they were the only people who had done the honourable thing'.[1] That sentiment would doubtless have been seconded by Communist miners' leader Arthur Horner, who had seen the swastika on his return to Wales from the besieged Republican citadel of Barcelona, then under heavy air bombardment from Franco's forces, with Condor Legion aircraft in the van. Horner told the *Western Mail* that 'To see the Nazi flag flying above the City-hall [sic] of the so-called capital of Wales is, I feel, a disgrace to the whole Welsh community'.[2]

Others took a very different view of the actions of Messrs McCale and Heginbottom. Speaking at a dinner engagement, the Lord

Mayor condemned their behaviour, claiming that 'there is such a thing to being a traitor to peace'. Major R. A. Hobbs told the same audience that 'they should not listen to fire-eaters, most of whom had done all they could to prevent Britain from being adequately armed'.[3] Defending his actions before the council, Purnell made it clear 'that he had no apology to make for flying the German flag', and that it had been flown 'not to support Nazi-ism [sic] but to show the world that they were anxious for the friendship of Germany'. He also pointed out that Swansea had celebrated Chamberlain's apparent diplomatic triumph in the same way.[4] Readers of the same issue of the *Western Mail* also learnt that officials of the Welsh League of Nations Union – a bastion of liberal-left opinion – had asked for it to be made clear that, contrary to some reports, 'no protest or objection as to the flying of the Swastika [sic] flag on the City-hall was made on their behalf by anybody'. A council employee duly returned the swastika to pride of place above Cardiff's civic centre. That moment was captured by a photographer, and the ensuing photograph can be seen on the cover of this book.

There are two reasons for using this cover image. The first is that the book focuses on the persistent accusation that one section of the Welsh population, namely Welsh nationalists, harboured Fascist sympathies; indeed, according to one of their most influential critics, that Plaid Cymru was 'the Fascist party in Wales'. This view appears to be deeply entrenched. Thus, for example, two recent widely-read and very well-received popular history potboilers, Richard Weight's *Patriots: National Identity in Britain 1940–2000* and Nick Groom's *Union Jack: The Story of the British Flag*, claim that Plaid Cymru sent an official delegation to Berlin in 1940.[5]

The claim is wholly baseless: nothing of the kind ever happened. We may (rightly) bemoan the scandalous lack of respect for basic scholarly standards that allowed such a damaging and false allegation to be circulated without an attempt at justification; in neither case is the allegation even referenced. But it is also important to ask why it was that such a claim must have appeared at least superficially plausible to the authors and their respective publishers. The answer to that puzzle, I would suggest, is that the claim that Welsh nationalists had at least some Fascist inclinations or sympathies has now been so consistently repeated that it requires no justification: it is held by many as a simple, self-evident truth. This accusation has been accepted and reproduced time and again; this book constitutes the first systematic attempt at examining and weighing the evidence.

The second reason for using the photograph is quite simply the way in which it jars with our contemporary sensibilities and expectations. Until confronted with the image, most people – of my acquaintance, at least – not only recoil (understandably) from the idea of the swastika being raised above the Welsh capital, they find it hard to imagine or accept that such a thing could ever have occurred. But it did, and this in turn should remind us of the precarious nature of much of what we call 'history'.

What we understand as the past – even and perhaps especially, the recent past – turns out on closer examination to be an often unsettling combination of truth, half-truth and downright untruth, a product of myth-making and forgetting quite as much as memory and remembrance. The task of scholarship is to seek to untangle these various strands whilst accepting, of course, that the final word will never be written. In the present case, the task of evaluating and making sense of the accusation of Fascism against Welsh nationalism is rendered easier by the fact that, for my generation at least, neither the dramatis personae nor the events in question were personally known or experienced. Viewing this controversy from a critical distance should now surely be possible. That, at least, is the spirit in which this book has been written.

* * *

This preface is the only part of the following book to have been written originally in English. Translating the rest from its original Welsh has served to remind me both of the incredible riches of the two languages, but also of the enormous differences between them. To state the case with a crudity that will no doubt make linguists wince, Welsh and English 'work' so very differently! The translation seeks to keep at least some of the original's flavour whilst ensuring that the work is as readable as possible in its new linguistic context.

Only others can judge how successfully the latter goal has been attained. But, to the extent that it has, it is largely down to the generous assistance of others. Dafydd Jones produced a first draft of the translation with amazing alacrity. My good friends and colleagues Roger Scully and Emyr Lewis helped smooth remaining rough edges in each successive draft. I am also grateful to suggestions from Ceri Davies, Lucy Hammond, Sarah Lewis, Wynn Thomas and Lisa Turnbull. Any remaining lack of fluency is, alas, solely my own responsibility.

Other debts have been incurred whilst producing this translated version of the text. As well as being strikingly efficient, colleagues at the University of Wales Press have been unfailingly enthusiastic about the project. I would like to thank, in particular, Helgard Krause and, again, Sarah Lewis and Dafydd Jones. I am also grateful to Adam Evans, Ken Jones, Rob Stradling and Chris Williams for their advice and assistance.

Richard Wyn Jones
January 2014

Notes

[1] *Western Mail*, 4 October 1938.
[2] *Western Mail*, 3 October 1938.
[3] *Western Mail*, 3 October 1938.
[4] *Western Mail*, 4 October 1938.
[5] Richard Weight, *Patriots: National Identity in Britain 1940–2000* (London: Macmillan, 2002), p. 49: 'Plaid Cymru . . . [sent] an official delegation to Berlin in the summer of 1940 to convince Hitler that in return for some measure of Welsh independence they would support a Nazi regime elsewhere on the island.' Nick Groom, *Union Jack, the Story of the British Flag* (London: Atlantic 2005) p. 266: 'disgracefully, the Welsh Nationalists went so far as to send an official delegation to Berlin in 1940'. I am grateful to Ken Jones for drawing these works to my attention.

Introduction

It is difficult, if not impossible, to imagine a more damaging accusation to make against any democratic politician or political party than to accuse them of being 'Fascist'. During the second half of the twentieth century, Fascism came to be regarded as representing the nadir of human history. In the Nazi concentration and extermination camps – Auschwitz, Bergen-Belsen . . . the roll-call is chillingly familiar – Fascists descended to depths of depravity that are beyond imagination. Notwithstanding the innumerable atrocities committed in the name of Stalin, of Mao or on behalf of the various empires constructed by European imperialism, Fascism occupies a unique position in contemporary understandings of evil. Indeed it is surely no exaggeration to say that, in this secular age, Hitler has come to embody Absolute Evil. To make a serious accusation that someone is a Fascist is to identify them with all of this.

The popular image of Plaid Cymru in its early years is not easily reconciled with our image of Fascists and Fascism.[1] Pacifist Nonconformist ministers, school teachers, college lecturers and various varieties of cultural nationalist appear to have little or nothing in common with thugs in jackboots and monochrome shirts – the uniform of the Fascist party meetings that proliferated throughout Europe in the interwar years. Yet time and again since the mid-1930s, the claim has been made that the Welsh Nationalist Party was a Fascist party. These accusations have been made by individuals of real substance whose opinions we would normally expect to take seriously – Cabinet ministers, members of Parliament, university principals, ministers of religion, and so on. There are some famous names among them, not least the first Secretary of State for Wales and one time Deputy Leader of the Labour Party, James Griffiths. Moreover the accusation is still repeated up to the present day.

This short book will explore these accusations and attempt a definitive accounting of the relationship between Plaid Cymru and Fascism. The stakes, I would contend, are high. If there is any objective basis for the accusation of Fascism against the party, we will be obliged to revise our entire understanding of the history of Plaid Cymru – and, indeed, of Welsh politics more generally. For if the accusation is substantiated, we will have to consider the implications of the 'fact' that a significant proportion of the Welsh intellectual class – almost certainly including the majority of Welsh speakers in their midst – have supported and even participated in a 'Fascist' party. We will have to wrestle with the implications of the 'fact' that a party that formed part of the Welsh Government between 2007 and 2011 is a party tainted by Fascist associations. Indeed, if the charges are substantiated, not only would our understanding of Welsh politics require fundamental revision: so too would our understanding of British politics. Rather than viewing Fascism as a largely 'continental' phenomenon, we would have to come to terms with the 'fact' that there is at least one corner of Britain where a Fascist-tinged or Fascist-influenced movement has managed to set down deep and tenacious roots. Plaid Cymru will need to be considered alongside the *Front National* in France, the *Freiheitspartei* in Austria, and those other parties normally accorded a central place in debates on the continuing influence of Fascism and neo-Fascism on contemporary European politics.

If on the other hand, this extremely serious accusation proves to be unfounded, it is appropriate that we consider what its regular, authoritative reproduction and repetition tells us about the nature of Welsh politics and political culture. Why is it that some of this country's most prominent politicians have seen fit to traduce the reputation of Plaid Cymru in such a way, even when the party posed very little objective threat to them? What is it about Plaid Cymru that has seemed to warrant such treatment? Why, furthermore, have political commentators consistently given the accusers free rein to spread such poisonous and insidious views about their opponents?

This interrogation of the relationship between Plaid Cymru and Fascism will be presented in five chapters. Initially we will examine 'The Accusations' directed at Plaid Cymru. This will be followed by a discussion of the complexities of 'Recognising Fascists and Fascism'; that leads, in turn, to an attempt at 'Defining Fascism' in order to establish criteria against which we can assess the political philosophy of Plaid Cymru so that we might determine the validity or otherwise of the repeated accusations made against it. Having examined and assessed the substance of the accusations, we will then turn to consider the question of why they have been repeated with such apparent conviction for so many years? There are two parts to the response. 'Wales during a decade of war' examines Plaid Cymru's attitudes and standpoints towards the Spanish Civil War and the Second World War. This precedes a broader consideration of 'Welsh Political Culture'.

* * *

This discussion of the accusation of Fascism against Plaid Cymru was originally intended for inclusion in the forthcoming second volume of my broader study of the party's political ideas (Volume 1, *Rhoi Cymru'n Gyntaf: Syniadaeth Plaid Cymru*, was published in 2007). My good friend Jerry Hunter was the first to suggest that it might stand alone as a separate volume. His suggestion was enthusiastically seconded by a number of other friends who were generous enough to read the text and offer their thoughts. I am indebted to Guto Harri, Emyr Lewis, Dafydd Trystan, John Stevenson, Daniel G. Williams and, of course, to Jerry for their comments. Staff at the University of Wales Press have been hugely supportive of the project since it was first suggested to them, and I would like to thank in particular Director Helgard Krause, Head of Commissioning Sarah Lewis, Production Manager Siân Chapman, and the Editor of the Press Dafydd Jones for their professionalism, patience and valuable suggestions. I am also grateful to the University of Wales Press's anonymous readers who provided further helpful comments on the manuscript.

In addition to the aforementioned, I have benefited enormously from suggestions and comments on earlier drafts of the text. My thanks, therefore, go to Meredydd Evans, Simon Brooks, Gwenan Creunant and R. Geraint Gruffydd. Peter Jackson, who has now departed Wales to settle in the old *Ystrad Clud*, has always been ready to share his encyclopaedic knowledge of the vast historiographical literature on European politics of the 1930s. Mike Williams, now of the University of Ottawa, was the third participant in our endlessly stimulating discussions about the political thought of the period. I have learnt a huge amount from both. My thanks also to Aled Elwyn Jones and Matthew Rees for sourcing materials, and to Lucy Hammond, Lee Waters and Peter Keelan for their assistance. I am grateful for the support of my colleagues at the Wales Governance Centre at Cardiff University, with thanks to Rebecca Rumbul and to Roger Scully in particular.

If there is any virtue to the discussion that follows, then much of the credit for that must go to the aforementioned. As the contents of this slim volume are likely to prove contentious, it is of even greater importance than usual that I clearly state at the outset that none of them are responsible for any flaws that remain. Responsibility for those is, unfortunately, entirely my own.

Richard Wyn Jones
Fagerstrand, Nesodden, Norway

Notes

[1] Plaid Genedlaethol Cymru/The Welsh Nationalist Party was founded during the winter of 1924/5. After 1945, the party became known as Plaid Cymru. In 1998, the party adopted the bilingual name Plaid Cymru – The Party of Wales. In 2006, the name was shortened to Plaid as part of a more general rebranding (although Plaid Cymru – The Party of Wales remained the party's official name). As the original Welsh-language version of this book was being completed, it was announced that the party would revert to the naming system that

existed during its first twenty years of existence and adopt different names in Welsh and English – Plaid Cymru / The Party of Wales. Only time will tell if the latest change takes root, but here I have used Plaid Cymru and Welsh Nationalist Party interchangeably.

1

The Accusations

The 25 November 1938 edition of the *Cambrian News*, in a column titled 'UCW Notes' reporting on life at what was then the University College of Wales, Aberystwyth, included the following snippet:

> A debate was held on Friday, the motion being 'That Welsh Nationalism is Welsh Nazi-ism.' The speakers were: For, R. Islwyn Pritchard and Edgar Jones; Against, G. I. Lewis and Dyfnallt Morgan. The motion was passed by a narrow margin.[1]

Too much significance should not be attached to the outcome of student debates.[2] On this occasion at least, however, the discussion – and its conclusion – reflected a broader reality. By 1938, the Welsh Nationalist Party was under siege from accusations of Fascism, or of Fascist sympathies, which were being levelled against it from many quarters.[3]

The form that such accusations took varied greatly: from throwaway remarks by authors who made no attempt to justify their accusations, to more sustained attempts to engage with specific aspects of the party's political ideas and positions. In the pre-war period, however, what is consistently apparent is that the seriousness of the accusations being levelled is inversely proportionate to the amount of evidence being marshalled to support them. Or, in other words, the more sweeping, defamatory and damaging the attacks, the more casual and slight the attempts at justification. Consider, for example, the charge laid by a *Daily Herald* correspondent writing on 15 February 1938: '"The Welsh Nationalist leaders are out and out Fascists, despite the fact that they try to hide it," said an ex-Nationalist to me . . .'.[4] No evidence whatsoever is offered in support of this claim beyond the words of an alleged 'source', identified only as an unnamed 'ex-Nationalist'.

During the 1930s, the Left displayed an increasing tendency to characterise opposing viewpoints as 'Fascist' without any great concern for accuracy – a tendency that, of course, continues to surface even today. As will be discussed later, such indiscriminate mud-slinging undoubtedly left its mark on the wider perception of Plaid Cymru, and is thus of political significance. But even more significant for the purposes of the present discussion are the more considered accusations that were levelled, not least those made by individuals who were in many respects extremely supportive of the party's aims.[5] In this context, perhaps the most significant critic in the years immediately preceding the Second World War was Prosser Rhys, editor of *Baner ac Amserau Cymru*, a man who had joined the party even before the famous founding meeting at Pwllheli in 1925 had taken place.[6] Rhys did not consider the party itself to be Fascist. But he did believe that those columns in the party's publications that focused on contemporary international developments such as the Spanish Civil War, were unwilling to utter 'an unkind word about Fascism'. Rhys believed that this was not only a monumental misunderstanding of what was at stake in current European politics, but was also contrary to the views of the party's rank and file members:

> The majority of Plaid members have Radical tendencies – Left wing tendencies if you will. Many joined the Nationalist Party from the Labour Party, many from the Liberal Party, with the majority of the remainder having no party affiliation but holding clearly Radical views. No one from among the disciples of Lord Rothermere and *Daily Mail* have joined the party, yet, to a degree, the attitude of the *Daily Mail* is the one adopted in Plaid journals on issues other than the domestic problems of Wales. This is contrary to the sympathies of the majority of the party's members.[7]

Rhys was therefore not accusing Plaid Cymru of being a Fascist party per se. Indeed, he was quite clear in his view that the vast majority of party members tended towards the political Left. What he did claim, however, was that views expressed in party periodicals on international affairs signally failed to support democratic elements in countries threatened by Fascism – from within or without.

It would seem that in due course Prosser Rhys revised his position regarding Plaid Cymru's stance on international affairs. At the outbreak of war, *Baner ac Amserau Cymru* and its editor stood as one with the party in calling upon Wales to adopt a neutral position and to support 'peace through compromise', that is to say peace without outright victory for one side or the other. Saunders Lewis's weekly column 'Cwrs y Byd' featured almost invariably on the front page of *Baner ac Amserau Cymru*, providing a platform from which Lewis could boldly and implacably expound his and his party's views on the war. Indeed many party members considered 'Cwrs y Byd' to have played a key role in ensuring the survival of Plaid Cymru during the difficult war years.[8] Whether or not this is true, the controversial opinions expressed in Lewis's column were without doubt provocative, if not inflammatory, insofar as those hostile to the party were concerned, and they certainly helped to ensure that accusations of Fascism continued to gain momentum.

During the war years, three notable attacks were mounted on Plaid Cymru by leading figures in Wales. The first to enter the fray was D. Emrys Evans, who had been Principal of the University College of North Wales (today's Bangor University) since 1927. In an essay published in the Summer 1941 issue of *Y Llenor*, entitled 'Y Rhyfel a'r Dewis' (The War and the choice'), Evans set about chastising the Welsh intelligentsia for its lukewarm support for the British cause during the war. The core of his argument was that politics had to deal with the real rather than the abstract or the fanciful, and given the conditions of 1941, Plaid Cymru's position of neutrality in relation to the war was neither credible nor sustainable. Those in Wales who refused to back the Allies were guilty, in Evans's opinion, of 'strengthening the cause of Fascist dictators'.[9] The nationalists, he believed, gave the impression that they were little more than 'a coalition of contrarians whose Zealot-like opposition to the English had blinded them to the ways in which the devastation of war had changed the world, and to the fact that the concerns of a party and nation mattered less than the fundamental rights of man'.[10] A Nazi victory would inevitably lead to the destruction of Welsh-language high culture because freedoms of speech and of expression were prerequisite to the latter's very existence. Welsh popular culture would also suffer. It is interesting and instructive to note the way in which the author's anti-Catholic prejudices surface in this context:

> How could the traditional popular culture of Wales expect to be treated under Nazism? If the Nazis ever soften in their position on religion, rest assured that it is to the Pope and the Roman Catholic Church that they will turn, towards a Catholic religion that is responsive to the general, catholic order that they intend to impose upon the nations. Any culture rooted in the traditions of liberal Nonconformity will get short shrift.[11]

The essay closed with the following somewhat portentous words, aimed directly at the Plaid Cymru leadership: 'Will the observer remain with his telescope in his tower, even though its foundations are besieged? Has he become so inflexible that he is unable to alter its focus even though the mist has hidden familiar terrain? Will we hear again of the treason of men of letters?'[12]

The allegations made by Evans were serious indeed (hatred of the English had led to treason), but he was accusing Plaid Cymru of consorting with Fascism rather than accusing it of being a Fascist party in its own right. The following year, however, the pressure escalated – as did the seriousness of the accusations – with two further attacks on the party.

In a St David's Day speech to the Cardiff Cymmrodorion Society in 1942, Thomas Jones (or T.J. as he was known) presented the following dramatic picture of the state of the nation:[13]

> In Wales the disappointment with the working of democracy in Parliament and in the county and local councils, and the breakdown of the Puritan framework and the communal power of the churches, has left a void into which the Blaid has entered with a new, narrow and intolerant dogma, and the vision of a new Promised Land of Fascism.[14]

There was little real substance to the argument: it was more a string of allegations, non-sequiturs and, indeed, threats than an attempt at rational argumentation. Plaid Cymru's objective of gaining dominion status for Wales meant, in his opinion, 'passports at Newport and tariffs along Offa's Dyke'. This would in due course lead to civil war because 'as dear as Wales is to many of us there are some things that are dearer to us. . . If we are forced to make a choice we shall fight for reason, for freedom, and the British Commonwealth as a stepping stone to world unity and citizenship.' As to why T.J. considered it justifiable to describe the party as a Fascist party, here is his argument *in toto*:

> At present its [the party's] tactics are to try and conciliate and exploit various movements which are not identified with it, the Urdd, the movement for adult education, the labour movement. It has recently become especially enamoured of the Urdd, it has discovered Denmark and Grundtvig, it promises to hand over the industries of South Wales to the workers. It will offer every thing to everybody provided sooner or later they will speak Welsh. This is all part of the Hitlerian technique.[15]

This is such a weak argument that it is impossible to take it seriously. Not least because if seeking support though promising of all manner of things to a varied constituency amounts to Hitlerism, then democratic politics *tout court* would be condemned as an expression of Fascism.

T.J. was an exceptionally gifted, intelligent man. Yet despite his academic bent, and his pioneering efforts to bring sophisticated and rigorous research work to bear on Wales's myriad social problems, he clearly felt no compulsion to offer any evidence in support of his accusation of Fascism against Plaid Cymru. This in no way detracts from the significance of his comments, however, because as he well knew, they were assured of a serious reception thanks to his particular status in the nation's life. He ranked, without question, among the most prominent and respected Welshmen of his day, and was a figure of real substance in British political life. Having risen from humble beginnings in the Rhymney valley to serve under four British prime ministers as Deputy Secretary to the Cabinet, T.J. represented and embodied the Welsh liberal and nationalist (with a small 'n') tradition at its most successful. Moreover, his devotion and loyalty to the land of his fathers was clear for all to see. Whether or not it was substantiated by any evidence, the charge of Fascism from this quarter was a significant blow to the Welsh Nationalist Party.

What is particularly ironic about T.J.'s accusation is that he had himself been (wrongly) accused only a few years previously of harbouring Fascist sympathies. He had been among those who supported in word and deed the policy of appeasement with Nazi Germany.[16] From December 1934 onwards, he had sought to use his considerable influence on the prime minister Stanley Baldwin to press for appeasement. Indeed, such was his desire to appease Hitler that in 1936 he held a series of private discussions with Germany's ambassador to Britain, Joachim von Ribbentrop. T.J. even travelled to Berlin and spent a weekend at the von Ribbentrop residence – from where he was taken to meet the Führer himself at the latter's own Berlin apartment. Later in the same year, he travelled again to Germany to meet Hitler, this time in the company of Lloyd George. He also sought other means to build bridges with Germany. Most striking, perhaps, was the occasion, again in 1936, when together with the editor of the *The Times*, Geoffrey Dawson, he pressed Eton College to offer a place to von Ribbentrop's son: an episode that speaks eloquently to the willingness of the British establishment – and the Welsh establishment in the form of T.J. – to extend a conciliatory hand to Nazi Germany.[17]

In the view of T.J. and other supporters of appeasement, an accommodation between Britain and Hitler was possible if the Foreign Office in London could be persuaded to switch from its traditional support for France and offer Germany less harsh conditions of (post 1914–18 War) reparation. He shared the assumptions of many in 1930s Britain that the root of the problem was the punitive conditions imposed on Germany by the Treaty of Versailles. Peace was possible if that wrong was righted. It was not until September 1938 that T.J. began to view the Nazis for what they really were. By that time, however, he had had to endure the experience of being branded as part of an establishment clique of

Fascist sympathisers, in a devastating and influential portrait penned by the Communist journalist Claud Cockburn.[18] There was no truth in the allegation. It is certainly the case that some members of the British establishment – such as Lord Londonderry, a cousin of Churchill's and heir to the family that gave Machynlleth its clock – strayed well over the boundary that separated appeasement from outright admiration, even adulation, for the Fascists and their aims.[19] Nevertheless, although T.J. and his associates were appallingly naïve – with T.J. himself guilty of hubristic arrogance in his belief that his own amateurish diplomatic efforts could somehow tame Hitler – they were no Fascists. It is also fair to acknowledge T.J.'s efforts to provide succour and support for Jewish refugees fleeing Germany.[20] Nonetheless despite the fact that T.J. was felt personally hurt by the unfair accusations made against him and his associates by Cockburn and others, he clearly felt no compunction about using the same tactics to attack Plaid Cymru. For him it seems that undermining the party's influence was part of the war effort.

By far the most widely known attack on Plaid Cymru for its alleged Fascist sympathies was that launched by the Reverend Gwilym Davies in his essay 'Cymru Gyfan a'r Blaid Genedlaethol Gymreig' (The Whole of Wales and the Welsh Nationalist Party), published as the lead article in the July 1942 issue of *Y Traethodydd*.[21] This essay constituted a no-holds-barred assault on the party, written by a man who had made a name for himself between the world wars as a promoter of peace not only in Wales but also at the home of the League of Nations in Geneva. A reminder of his status is that he was the initiator of the 'Message of Peace and Goodwill from the young people of Wales to the young people of the World'.[22] Once again, here was an individual who both represented and embodied the ideals of liberal Nonconformist Wales.

This was the most detailed of the attacks mounted against Plaid Cymru in this period, and was the only one to make any attempt to refer to the party's policy agenda in support of the accusation that it was a Fascist party. For this reason, Gwilym Davies's arguments deserve close scrutiny. They may be summarised as follows.

The party's social and moral ideas stemmed from Catholicism, specifically from the 1891 *Rerum Novarum* and the 1931 *Quadragesimo Anno* Papal Encyclicals. But, unlike the Catholic parties of the continent, Plaid Cymru was unprepared to work with other parties, because of the debt that it owed 'in policy and stance to *L'Action Française* and to M. Charles Maurras'.[23] Because if Rome was the source of the party's social and moral ideas, then its political ideas derived from Maurras and *L'Action Française*. In Davies's view, Maurras was 'the father of Fascism as a political system'.[24] The aim of Maurras and his fanatical paramilitary footsoldiers, the *Camelots du Roi*, was to 'free France from any democratic influence, to restore the country to a totalitarian monarchy, purely "fascist" in its political organisation, and to preserve it as wholly Papist'.[25] Maurras achieved his great victory with 'the fall of the Third Republic in France in June 1940'.[26] Pétain's Vichy France – the Nazis' docile pet state – was by 1942 being governed in a manner that was entirely consistent with Maurras's ideas.

What fate would befall Wales if the Welsh Nationalist Party was ever to assume power? Consistent with the party's influences, Wales would become an 'independent, totalitarian, fascist and papist' country.[27] Independent because 'That is what . . . Dominion Status means, – the right for Wales to be entirely independent of England in all its political and economic organisation'.[28] Totalitarian because 'if the Nationalist Party is to be the only party in an independent Wales, then Wales will be a totalitarian country'.[29] Fascist because 'the difference between fascism and democracy in any country is the form that its parliament' assumes, and Plaid Cymru wanted a Welsh Parliament to take on a Fascist form.[30] Proof of Plaid Cymru's aim to create a Papist Wales was to be found in Saunders Lewis's emphasis on '"re-establishing", – not establishing, "re-establishing" – in Wales a "Welsh Christian State"'.[31]

In order to achieve Plaid Cymru's aim, 'Without doubt, after the war – and it would not surprise me to know that this was already in motion – hundreds of young Welshmen will be recruited to some sort of *Camelots du Roi* . . . in the name of Plaid Cymru.'[32] Yet in Wales, any such initiative was bound to fail; it would rather divide the country and destroy any hope of a national future.

Lest there remain the slightest ambiguity, Davies's essay concluded with the following words: 'Great is the responsibility of the leaders of the Welsh Nationalist Party or, not to beat around the bush, the Fascist Party in Wales.'[33]

As far as the internal logic of his argument goes, Gwilym Davies's comments regarding the influence of Catholicism on Plaid Cymru's social and moral ideas were in truth neither here nor there. They were certainly not necessary in order for the essay to ascend to its rousing crescendo. Their rhetorical fuction was, however, critical. The aim was to prey on the anti-Catholic prejudices of a Welsh Nonconformist readership – prejudices that had made life difficult for the party ever since Saunders Lewis had announced in the early 1930s that he had himself been received into the Roman Catholic Church.[34] Davies's less than subtle suggestion was that Plaid Cymru had fallen victim to suspect foreign influences, and that the party was set on a course that would lead to those influences corrupting the Welsh way of life. A logic parallel to Davies's was, of course, not unknown in Europe at this time – even if it was not most immediately associated with the anti-Fascist cause.

Davies's argument regarding the alleged Fascist nature of Plaid Cymru contained two elements – one implicit, the other explicit.

1. *Implicit*: that Charles Maurras, the 'father of Fascism', was the dominant influence on Plaid Cymru's political thought; ergo Plaid Cymru was a Fascist party.
2. *Explicit*: that Fascist ideas were central to the Nationalists' programme for the future of Wales. Specifically, (i) the party intended to found a one-party state in Wales, and (ii) the nature of the political institutions that the party proposed for an 'Independent' Wales was Fascist. Plaid Cymru would also adopt Fascist methods after the war by creating a paramilitary wing.

What evidence did Davies present in support of his argument?[35]

As far as the implicit case was concerned, Davies noted that Ambrose Bebb, a prominent early member of the Welsh National Party, had enthusiastically praised Maurras on numerous occasions in his published essays. This was undeniably true. But, as Davies also had to concede, Bebb had distanced himself from Plaid Cymru during the war years because he disagreed with the party's support for neutrality, arguing that the barbarism of Nazi Germany had to be opposed by force. Reference to Bebb alone was hardly sufficient.[36] Rather, Saunders Lewis had somehow to be shepherded into the Fascist fold; after all, 'one cannot think of Saunders Lewis without thinking of the Welsh Nationalist Party. Since 1926, he has been its leader, and he is its hero.'[37] However, as any references to Maurras in Lewis's work were scarce, Davies could only resort to a prime example of sophistry:

> The book *Tradition and Barbarism: A Survey of Anti-Romanticism*, by Professor P. Mansell Jones of Bangor, provides an excellent description of the French movement along with a fair assessment of the place and importance of Maurras in French literary life. In his preface, Professor P. M. Jones thanks Mr Saunders Lewis for proof-reading his work and for prompting him to discuss some of the topics of French literature.[38]

Put simply, Davies 'proves' Maurras's influence on the political thought of Plaid Cymru by establishing that a close acquaintance of Saunders Lewis had published a book that discussed aspects of French cultural life, which included Maurras, and had acknowledged in the preface Lewis's help and encouragement. Were it not for the fact that the accusation was such a serious one, the crudity – indeed, the *chutzpah* – of this attempt to smear the party would render it laughable.

Reverend Davies became even more deeply mired in intellectual dishonesty in his attempt to demonstrate that specific aspects of Plaid Cymru policies were fascist. He offered no evidence whatsoever in support of his allegation that the party would seek to found a single-party dictatorship in Wales, and for a very simple reason: the allegation was false. Indeed, among the most prominent themes in Saunders Lewis's wartime journalism was the need to allow for differences in opinion precisely as a defence against totalitarianism. Reference to Plaid Cymru's alleged wish to create a paramilitary wing was equally untrue. There was no evidence or basis for making such a claim. Indeed the very idea that a party made up of more than its fair share of ministers and trainee ministers of religion, teachers and college lecturers – very many of whom were pacifists – was intent on creating a thuggish paramilitary wing along the lines of the *Camelots du Roi* is patently absurd.

Allowing that we might for a moment accept Davies's quite bizarre suggestion that the difference between Fascist and democratic states revolves around the organisation of the legislature, then in this regard he did provide at least some evidence in support of the argument that Plaid Cymru's objective was to institute a Fascist political order. In an essay on trade unions published in *Y Ddraig Goch* in 1932, Saunders Lewis had called for trade union representation in the second chamber of any Welsh parliament.[39] According to Gwilym Davies, this exposed the true colours of Saunders Lewis and his party, because 'That is the fascist form of a parliament, a form that acknowledges the right of trade unions to representation, but that refuses completely the right of the individual as citizen to vote and the rights of the people in the polling station.'[40] Davies's version, however, was a complete misrepresentation of Lewis. Believing that at least some members of a legislature's second chamber should be selected in order to represent the interests of a particular group does not amount to Fascism. What has been termed 'functional representation' is a familiar feature of many democratic parliaments. Bishops continue to sit in the House of Lords, the second chamber of the United Kingdom. Of even greater relevance in the present context given the influence of Irish nationalism in Plaid Cymru, is that functional representation (including trade union representation) is a feature of the *Seanad Éireann*, the second chamber in Ireland.[41] But even this is only a secondary issue. What was most striking about Davies's interpretation is the leap he makes from Lewis's support for trade union representation in a Welsh second chamber to the allegation that advocating such representation was tantamount to a denial of the citizen's right to vote. Lewis had suggested nothing of the sort. Rather Lewis and his party were consistent in their support for a Welsh parliament with a directly-elected lower chamber. In order to justify his accusation of Fascism, Davies was guilty of distorting the facts beyond all recognition. Indeed, Davies's entire essay is an exercise in brass-necked, bare-faced dissimulation; or more colloquially, in lying.

Some Plaid Cymru supporters believed that the attacks mounted upon it were the result of a conspiracy to undermine their party and its leadership. A. O. H. Jarman suggested as much in a retrospective piece he wrote reflecting on the party's expriences during the war years: 'without doubt, there was a concerted campaign to oppose the influence of Saunders Lewis and to besmirch his reputation'. The chief orchestrator of this campaign, in Jarman's view, was Thomas Jones.[42] T.J. was without doubt an influential man, and there can be equally little doubt that by 1941 he regarded the Welsh Nationalist Party as a major irritant as a result of the position that the party had taken on the war. We now know that T.J. encouraged Geoffrey Dawson – his fellow lobbyist in the cause of a place for Ribbentrop's son at Eton – to mount a libel case against *Baner ac Amserau Cymru* based on an isolated reference in it to *The Times*. Honour was ultimately satisfied with an editorial correction.[43] It is clear also that T.J. sought to prevent Lewis's appointment to a committee assembled to consider plans for post-war Wales.[44] In addition, he organised publication of the pamphlet series *Pamffledi Harlech*, which featured essays far less critical of the war than the views being voiced by Saunders Lewis in *Baner ac Amserau Cymru*. Neither can we ignore the suggestive comment made by T.J. to Dawson to the effect that he was 'taking one or two other steps to counter . . . [Plaid Cymru's] mischief, of which you will hear more by the by'.[45] It is at the very least possible, then, that behind the scenes he encouraged attacks such as those made by Emrys Evans and Gwilym Davies.

I shall not attempt here to prove or disprove the existence of any conspiracy or 'concerted campaign'. Yet, despite Gwilym Davies's dismissal as mere 'claptrap' any suggestion that he was operating under T.J.'s influence,[46] there remains sufficient evidence to indicate (at the very least) a sustained level of dialogue and collaboration in the higher echelons of the Welsh establishment surrounding the attempt to tar Plaid Cymru with the brush of Fascism. This dialogue extended to some of Wales's main cultural and spiritual institutions. Gwilym Davies received advice and encouragement from Edgar Jones, Alun Oldfield-Davies and Hopkin Morris, a prominent triumvirate at the head of the BBC in Wales.[47] Indeed, the first of these three commented – on the corporation's own headed note-paper, no less – on a draft of the text that would later be published in *Y Traethodydd*. Davies was also advised by G. A. Edwards, Principal of the Theological College in Aberystwyth.[49] Also note-worthy is the fact that the Nonconformist denomination that published *Y Traethodydd* – the Welsh Calvinistic Methodists – decided to publish Davies's essay as a separate off-print in addition to making it the lead essay in the periodical itself.[50] This, we might surmise, in order to maximise its readership.

Conspiracy or not, what is most significant for the purposes of the present discussion is how the surviving correspondence between the accusers and their supporters reveals the central role that anti-Catholicism played in shaping the attacks on Plaid Cymru. In a letter to one of the editors of *Y Traethodydd* following the publication of 'Cymru Gyfan', Davies described his ambition for the essay in the following terms: 'If it helps to save Wales from being under-mined by Roman Catholic propaganda I shall feel it will have done some good.'[51] Much of the Nonconformist response to the Plaid Cymru leadership during the period in question is summed up in comments made by that particular editor, D. Francis Roberts, in a letter he wrote to Gwilym Davies. Referring to J. E. Daniel, who published a defence in reply to Davies's attack, Roberts makes the following aside:

> You know that his wife, the daughter of a Welsh Congregationalist Minister is a RC. I heard from a reliable source that their children were baptised in Garthewyn, Vale of Clwyd, the chapel (RC) where Mr Wynne, one of the stalwarts of the 'Blaid' attends.[52]

The daughter of a Congregational minister a Catholic – heaven forfend!

The accusations of Fascism peaked during the winter of 1942–3, and the bitter by-election campaign for the University of Wales parliamentary constituency.[53] In order to prevent any chance of victory for Saunders Lewis, the Plaid Cymru candidate and *bête noir* of the party's opponents, the Welsh establishment united behind the candidacy of Professor W. J. Gruffydd, editor of *Y Llenor* and a prominent figure in Welsh life – a man who had been vice-president of Plaid Cymru during the imprisonment of Saunders Lewis, D. J. Williams and Lewis Valentine in the aftermath of the burning of storage sheds at the site of a proposed RAF bombing school on the Llŷn Peninsula in 1936, and at that stage a very vocal supporter of their actions.[54] Gruffydd and his supporters presented the by-election as a battle between Reason and Freedom on the one hand,[55] and Reaction and Irrationalism on the other. Saunders Lewis's – and his party's – alleged sympathy with Fascism was central to Gruffydd's campaign. Once again, some of the allegations made were very crude indeed. Thus, according to the pseudonymous John Pennant writing in the *Western Mail*, Plaid Cymru was a Fascist party. Pennant claimed that Saunders Lewis's status within the party reflected 'a blind and blinding adulation that has no parallel since Adolph [sic] Hitler set up business as the "saviour of my people"'.[56] Another frequently made accusation was that if Lewis and his party were not actually Fascists themselves, then they were as good as being so, because in word and deed they gave succour to Britain's Fascist enemies on the continent. There could be no third way in this war: to refuse to support the Allies was to support the enemy.[57]

Yet again, anti-Catholicism was central to the arguments of Gruffydd's supporters; this in turn reflecting the strong anti-Catholic current in Welsh Nonconformity.[58] Time and again during the campaign Lewis was reproached for his Catholicism. Here, for example, is the editorial view propounded by *Seren Gomer*, the newspaper of the Welsh Baptists, on the eve of the election: 'If Mr Saunders Lewis is elected, I would not hesitate to say that there will be even greater rejoicing within the Roman Catholic Church than within the ranks of his own political supporters.'[59] Catholicism was not only viewed as mistaken on theological grounds; it was also considered by many as politically suspect because of its alleged affinities with Fascism. The latter view was surely part of the motivation for the following remarkable snippet that appeared in the 23 January 1943 edition of Y *Cymro*:

> We have received word . . . to inform us that the North Wales Communist Party has unanimously voted in favour of Professor W. J. Gruffydd, because, so it says, of his untiring work in support of Protestantism in the broadest sense, and in the belief that he will continue to fight for these things.[60]

If Communists in north Wales were atheists, then they were clearly Protestant atheists! The former judge Thomas Artemus Jones pulled even fewer punches in his intervention:

> the political philosophy of the Nationalists is . . . a patchwork of Fascist and Nazi capriciousness . . . It seeks to establish a Parliament in Wales that will not tolerate any other party except for the nationalists within its state, and a Government that will be Fascist and Papist.[61]

The assault mounted by Reverend Gwilym Davies had left its mark.

There can be no doubt that W. J. Gruffydd regarded Fascism and Catholicism as bedfellows. He considered both to be particular manifestations of a wider stream of Reaction and Irrationalism that was threatening the foundations of 'humanism and humanitarianism'. Gruffydd had already given expression to this Manichean worldview in an essay titled 'Mae'r gwylliaid ar y ffordd' (The barbarians are coming), published in Y *Llenor* in October 1940. There he identified the emergence of a 'conscious rebellion' against Progress and Development. Among the members of this rebel alliance he identified Nietzsche, Thomas Carlyle, *Action Française*, Hitler and Roman Catholicism. When it is recalled that this essay was written and published at a time when Hitler and Mussolini were at the zenith of their power, it is both striking and significant that Gruffydd devoted far greater attention to the role of France and Catholicism in the Reaction than he did to Nazism and Fascism. He was viciously critical of the Catholic church, even going so far as to suggest that there was some form of grand Catholic conspiracy at work in European politics:

For many years now, the clerical party in the Roman Catholic Church, that is, the party that would restore the *political* power of the Church, has been working with extraordinary energy to gain control of the Foreign Offices of different countries, particularly non-catholic counties . . . Outside of the Foreign Office, for instance, less than nine per cent of senior officials in Britain's civil service are Catholic; in the Foreign Office, it's over sixty per cent! Until recently, almost every British ambassador to the most important European states was a member of the Roman Catholic Church. In short, British diplomacy – and to a slightly lesser degree, American diplomacy – has fallen into the clutches of the Papists.[62]

In the next sentence, Gruffydd hints at the practical consequence of these circumstances:

Concurrent with this fact is another that is equally shocking – many of our ambassadors are supporters of Reaction, with some hoping to achieve 'an understanding' between Britain and Germany.[63]

Bluntly put, Gruffydd was suggesting that 'the appeasement policy about which so much was heard at the time of Mr Chamberlain' was actually a Catholic conspiracy.[64] Here we are confronted with the kind of green-ink conspiracy theorising that now proliferates on the internet.

W. J. Gruffydd did not believe that there were any fundamental, insurmountable differences between the various elements of the Reactionary coalition that he had identified. Yes, the Pope had condemned 'the barbarians' in the form of Hitler. But this condemnation was not motivated by humanitarian concerns: 'humanitarianism is not only absent from Papist Christianity, it is viewed with disdain by it.'[65] It was rather the failure of the Nazis to recognise the Church's special standing that had provoked papal condemnation. Such a state of affairs would not last:

To date, there is no public accord between Hitler and the Pope, and I venture that there will be no such accord until it is certain that Hitler will succeed in his plans for Europe. *And at that very moment, he will be reconciled with the Pope*, and Falbhauer [*sic*] and other persecuted Catholics will be instructed to toe the line drawn for them by the Pope.[66]

Although Reaction was discernible 'in more than one nation and in more than one intellectual circle',[67] its varied manifestations were united in their hostility towards Development, Progress, Reason and Freedom. And, with the waves of Reaction now crashing against the Welsh and British shoreline, Gruffydd concluded his essay with a warning about the enemy within: 'Above all else, we must remember that there are already men in this land who are poised, ready to open the floodgates, as they have already been opened in the Netherlands and Norway and France. Be warned and stand guard against Seithennin.'[68]

The target of Gruffydd's remarks were the leaders of Plaid Cymru, a fact that would have been patently obvious to anyone who had read his exchanges with Saunders Lewis in *Y Llenor* thirteen years before.[69] It would appear, however, that some misunderstood the piece, believing that Gruffydd was taking aim at pacifist opponents of the war. In order to ensure that there could be no misunderstanding, Gruffydd re-entered the fray. In his editorial comments for the winter issue of *Y Llenor*, he explicitly excluded the 'pasiffistiaid' from his criticism, and, again, took aim at the nationalists. 'If ever Hitler should come to Wales, who among the people of Wales will be chosen by him as his treacherous governors [*brad-raglofiaid*] to oversee the government of the country in line with the totalitarian principle?'[70] He answered his own question by declaring that the members of Plaid Cymru would be most prominent among them. Then, in a remarkable *ad hominem* attack on the party's president, J. E. Daniel, Gruffydd suggested that Daniel used his role as a lecturer at the Bala-Bangor Theological Seminary to poison the minds of Welsh Nonconformist ministerial candidates:

> If proclaiming Nationalism (a word and an idea that has been corrupted and debased and perverted for their own benefit by those who have oppressed the common people through the ages) gains precedence above Freedom and Humanitarianism in the future message of Congregationalists and Baptists, and if you [Daniel] are

responsible for that, then you will have succeeded in just a few years in undoing the devout work of the Nonconformist fathers over many centuries – and, in order to retain some semblance of religion in the land, the sooner the better these Nazified Congregationalists and Baptists find their way to the Church of Rome.[71]

In an echo of the Nazi tendency to equate Jewishness and Bolshevism, W. J. Gruffydd equated Catholicism to Fascism. Defeating both was part of a single struggle; and the representative of Catholicism and Fascism in Wales was Plaid Cymru.

It is difficult to overstate the bitterness of the by-election campaign, or the depth of the scars that it left. Paradoxically enough, one consequence of the vitriol heaped on Saunders Lewis's supporters was that it forged a sense of unity (in adversity) among them. Thus those commentators who have noted the importance of the campaign in reviving the spirits of Welsh nationalism are undoubtedly correct in their assessment.[72] Indeed, in more general terms, Plaid Cymru survived the war in a far better shape than one might have anticipated. Yet it is certainly the case that being branded as Fascist did significant, long-lasting damage to the party. It has been an albatross around its neck ever since.

It would be both tedious and pointless to seek to detail every attempt in the post-war years to remind the people of Wales of Plaid Cymru's alleged Fascism. But there was certainly nothing among them approximating the level of specificity to be found in the attacks of Gwilym Davies or even W. J. Gruffydd. It was rather a case of generalised insinuation and assertion. What is most significant is not the exact detail of the accusations, but the status of the accusers. The particular historical and political contexts of the accusations is also critical. The following may serve as representative examples.

Ness Edwards

In the course of his career as the long-serving Member of Parliament for Caerphilly, Ness Edwards also held the Cabinet position of

Postmaster General between 1950 and 1951 in the Attlee Government. During the 1945 election campaign, 'Ness Edwards reputedly displayed a Nazi lamp-shade made of human skin, warning his audience that Welsh Nationalists would commit similar atrocities once in power'.[73] After 1966, Edwards was among a group of Welsh Labour MPs who shunned Gwynfor Evans on account of his alleged 'Fascist' tendencies. Indeed, Edwards even refused to speak to the MP for Carmarthen.[74] At the by-election that followed Edwards's death – the celebrated Caerphilly by-election in 1968 – the accusation of Fascism against Plaid Cymru was part of Labour's rhetorical armoury as they fought to retain the constituency in the face of a swelling tide of support for the nationalists following Evans's landmark 1966 victory. Warning constituents against voting for Plaid Cymru, the eventually victorious Labour candidate, Fred Evans, claimed that 'Unless we are careful we shall have an incipient form of Fascism – a pernicious and evil thing for the future of Wales.'[75]

Jim Griffiths

During the 1950 general election, the following headline appeared in the *Western Mail*: 'Nazi Ideology of Plaid Cymru – Mr James Griffiths'.[76] While written by the paper's sub-editor, the headline was a concise summary of the content of a speech that Griffiths had delivered to an election meeting held in Burry Port. In it he claimed that the Welsh Republican Movement – a small but vocal organisation that came to prominence in late 1949 – harboured Nazi ideas.[77] Griffiths went on to claim that the Plaid Cymru candidate, the Reverend Eirwyn Morgan, was sympathetic towards the aspirations of the Republicans – *ergo* the 'Nazi Ideology of Plaid Cymru'.[78] During the Attlee government, Jim Griffiths was a member of the Cabinet as Secretary of State for the Colonies. He was also Deputy Leader of the Labour Party. In 1964 he was appointed the first Secretary of State for Wales.[79]

Leo Abse

Leo Abse was Member of Parliament for Pontypool from 1958 until 1987, and a highly respected backbencher – deservedly so in light of the wholly admirable role he played in ensuring progressive social reforms, such as the 1967 legislation that began to end legal discrimination against homosexuals. Abse played a prominent role as part of the No campaign for 1979 referendum on Welsh devolution, during which he raised the spectre of Hitlerism while opposing the aspirations of Welsh nationalists (be they of the small or large 'n' varieties):

> When high certitudes collapse, and faith becomes overcrowded with doubt, the resulting alienation in society can lead, as we know from the example of Nazi Germany, to regressive choices being made: the choices of xenophobia and Nineteenth Century Nationalism are being offered to us on March 1st.[80]

He may not have explicitly described the supporters of devolution as Nazis, but the inference is clear.

Kim Howells

Kim Howells pales in comparison to Leo Abse in terms of his political contribution, but as the Member of Parliament for Pontypridd between 1989 and 2010 he climbed far higher up the career ladder than the Member for Pontypool ever did. Howells served as a minister in several government departments during the Blair era. After leaving government, the position of this former-Communist trade union official at the heart of the British political establishment was underlined when he was appointed Chair of the UK Parliament's Intelligence and Security Committee overseeing the activities of the state's intelligence agencies.

Howells has never hidden his suspicion of the steps that have been taken towards establishing a measure of self-government for Wales. What is particularly interesting from the perspective of the present discussion are the arguments that he has used in expressing those suspicions. With devolution back on the agenda in the mid-1990s as a result of his own party's renewed commitment (to Scottish devolution, in particular), Howells drew attention to the nationalist agenda that he saw as 'lurking' behind devolution. Referencing the appalling conflicts – and resulting 'ethnic cleansing' – then unfolding in the former Yugoslavia, Howells warned that devolution would lead to 'the Balkanisation of Britain'.[81] Howells would go even further. In a subsequent interview given when he was Minister of State, and in reference to the Left-wing credentials of Plaid Cymru, he said: 'I'm never very sure that nationalism has got anything to do with socialism. I keep putting the words together and coming up with Hitler.'[82]

The Welsh Mirror *and the spectre of 'Fascist' and 'racist' nationalism*

In the wake of the success of Plaid Cymru in the first election to the National Assembly for Wales in 1999, the party found itself under constant attack, either directly or indirectly in the form of attacks on the national movement more generally. The party's 'Fascist' past was a key focus of these attacks, with this (supposed) legacy being directly linked with the party's and the Welsh language movement's (alleged) racism at the start of the twenty-first century. These were the constituent elements of what the *Welsh Mirror* termed the 'Hatred at the heart of Plaid' – a headline that was accompanied by a photograph of Saunders Lewis.[83]

The tabloid *Welsh Mirror*, a Welsh edition of the *Daily Mirror*, was established after the 'silent earthquake' of the May 1999 Assembly election in an attempt to steady and restore the fortunes of the Labour Party in Wales. At the time, the paper had the highest circulation of any newspaper in Wales. The consistent message of its political journalism was that Plaid Cymru and Welsh nationalism more generally were tainted with Fascism.[84] The newspaper's efforts were central to a broader Labour campaign to depict Plaid Cymru as a party of extremists, and thus to undermine the credibility of those political positions associated with it – particularly so the survival of the Welsh language and home rule. Few opportunities to put in the metaphoric boot were missed. In a parliamentary debate held in 2002, Wayne David claimed that there was a 'strong strand of racism and xenophobia in Plaid Cymru's history'. Referring to Saunders Lewis specifically, David claimed:

> He believed that he could embrace the corporatist ideas of Mussolini, with whom he was enamoured. He certainly had plenty of time for the racist remarks of various fascist elements arising in Europe in the 1920s and 1930s. Let me make it clear that he was an anti-Semite.[85]

Sixty years on from the University of Wales election, there was a period at the start of this century when the readers of the *Welsh Mirror* could have easily been forgiven for thinking Saunders Lewis was still alive and stalking the land.

The attacks on Plaid Cymru were, without doubt, extraordinarily crude – witness, for example, the *Welsh Mirror*'s political editor's claim that the actions of Welsh nationalists would lead in due course to 'people on cattle trucks on their way to concentration camps'.[86] But crudity is frequently a characteristic of the most effective propaganda. And Plaid Cymru's leadership conspicuously failed to find an effective riposte to the incessant claims that their movement was tainted by Fascism and the darkest days of the twentieth century. This was not the only reason why the party lost ground at the 2003 National Assembly elections. At the same time as these attacks were being launched against Welsh nationalism, Labour, rebranded as 'Welsh Labour', was reconnecting with the electorate as a party that was more positive in its embrace of Welsh identity and in its support for devolution. But there can be no doubt that Plaid Cymru suffered as a result of the accusations of Fascism that were such a prominent feature of the first term of the National Assembly for Wales.

In the wake of the May 2003 election, the *Welsh Mirror* ceased publication. Its work had been done.

2

Recognising Fascists and Fascism

Thus far, we have considered the range and variety of the accusations of Fascism made against Plaid Cymru; it might even be said that the attention they have been given is far greater than the accusations themselves warrant. But it is only through close examination than we can establish how feeble were the efforts to present supporting evidence. It is also only through sustained scrutiny that we become fully aware of the sophistry and crude anti-Catholic prejudice that riddled the meagre 'evidence' that was actually produced. It would be an obvious travesty to indict Plaid Cymru of harbouring Fascist sympathies on such an inadequate basis. Yet it does not automatically follow that we can dismiss the case against simply because the evidence put forward by the accusers is so manifestly inadequate. Bearing in mind the potentially explosive significance of the issue, we should at least consider the alleged 'Fascism' of Plaid Cymru from other perspectives.

In assessing whether there is any truth to the accusations made against the party, there is a preliminary question which must be answered, namely how are Fascists to be recognised? In other words, how would we know whether Plaid Cymru was a Fascist party, or had embraced Fascism in the past? What evidence would be sufficient to prove that the accusation was – or is – true? It is a far from simple question, however, because, as we shall see in due course, experts continue to debate fiercely about what constitutes Fascism and who should be counted as a Fascist. Indeed, such are the differences in opinion that there are some academics who would abandon use of the term entirely regarding it as analytically useless.

Such a response would, however, be neither adequate nor acceptable for our present purposes. To refuse to ask whether or not Plaid Cymru's past is tainted by Fascist sympathies because there is no universally agreed definition of Fascism would be facile. That is certainly not the way to address the fundamental questions posed in the opening paragraphs of the introduction to this book about the nature of Plaid Cymru and the political culture of Wales. We are required, therefore, to pursue a different, more holistic approach.

Let us proceed by first agreeing what *cannot* be considered as sufficient evidence that the ideas of an individual or political organisation can be considered as Fascist. It is quite clear that the existence of an accusation or accusations is not enough in itself enough to warrant a guilty verdict. As many commentators have noted – and as should indeed be obvious to all of us – the term 'Fascist' is frequently bandied about with scant regard for its accuracy or fairness. Indeed 'Fascist' has become a general insult to be thrown casually in the direction of traffic wardens, the tax authorities, politicans in whom we have become disillusioned, or football referees. In short, stronger evidence is required than simply the existence of an accusation.[1]

It must further be conceded at the outset that the occasional word of praise for a Fascist leader, or for a specific policy or policies enacted by a Fascist government, is also insufficient evidence to conclude that the author or the organisation that she or he represents should be thought of as Fascist. After all, there are few significant figures in interwar British politics who did *not*, at one time or another, make some statement or other with regards Fascism or Fascists that we would now consider to be naïve, ill-advised, or downright idiotic. To note only a handful of examples, consider the following description of Mussolini made in September 1935: 'So great a man . . . so wise a rule.' The words are those of Winston Churchill. In June 1937, he was again to declare, '[I]f I had been Italian, I should have been on Mussolini's side fifteen years ago.'[2] In a letter written in December 1937, Lloyd George described Hitler in similar vein as '[T]he great leader of a great people', before proclaiming that:

I have never doubted the fundamental greatness of Hitler, even in moments of profound disagreement with his policy . . . I have never withdrawn one particle of the admiration which I personally felt for him and expressed on my return from Germany.[3]

In view of the atrocities that had already been committed by Hitler and his party by 1937, Lloyd George might easily be accused of naïvety, arrogance and stupidity in his dealings with the dictator. But would we brand Lloyd George a Fascist? Hardly. And, similarly, to brand his party as such would be even more laughable. In the same vein, who in their right mind would describe Churchill or the party to which he belonged when he made his comments – the Conservative Party – as Fascist?

The political Left was considerably more resistant to the siren calls of Fascists and Fascism – the error of much of the interwar Left was to allow itself to become enamoured of Stalinism. Still, there is plenty of evidence that a large number of prominent members and supporters of the British Labour Party were naïve to the point of irresponsibility in their response to the rise of Fascism. The *New Statesman*, for example, supported the annexation of Sudetenland from Czechoslovakia in 1938 and argued for the further appeasement of Germany over the Danzig Corridor in 1939. Indeed, Britain's left-wing periodicals of the 1930s refused to support the closure of the Suez canal to Italian vessels following that country's attack on Abyssinia.[4] Even *Tribune*, with Aneurin Bevan on its editorial board, while enthusiastically supporting the Spanish Republic, opposed a British rearmament 'specifically geared to combating Fascism'.[5]

There is also ample evidence of admiration in progressive circles for specific social policies implemented by the Nazis as part of their programme to revive the country's economy in the aftermath of the Great Depression. In fact, if we scrutinise the politics of the 1930s in detail, we are hard pressed to find any serious intellect not mired in the disastrous economic orthodoxy of the day who did not take an active interest in at least some of the policy experiments being carried out in the Fascist states. With the social model characterised by free-market capitalism and parliamentary democracy having apparently exhausted itself on the killing fields of the First World War, and seeming to be impotent in the face of the subsequent economic devastation, there was a general desire for new ideas and successful examples that might be emulated.[6] And yet, whatever the family resemblance between some elements of Roosevelt's New Deal, for example, and Fascist policies, the proponents of the New Deal cannot themselves be considered Fascists.[7]

All of this reinforces the argument that far more substantial evidence than the occasional individual comment is required before it can be credibly argued that a particular individual or group is Fascist. Nevertheless, we are still left with the challenge of identifying more satisfactory grounds for deciding on the validity on any particular accusation.

One possibility worth considering is whether or not those who described themselves as Fascists acknowledged Plaid Cymru as some kind of kindred spirit. Were that to be the case, then this would provide us with at least some prima facie evidence that there might be more substance to the accusations than has so far been evident. After all, the many Fascist parties that emerged during the interwar years did acknowledge a certain kinship with each other; this despite their pseudo-Darwinian beliefs in competition between nations.[8] There is not a shred of evidence, however, that any of these parties ever recognised a familial similarity between themselves and the Welsh Nationalist Party.

Another related possibility is that those who can credibly claim expertise in the field – academics who have immersed themselves in the study of Fascism – have noticed some Fascist dimension to Plaid Cymru. The literature on Fascism is vast. Indeed it would appear that no Fascist party or organisation has escaped scholarly attention, no matter how minor or insignificant it might appear. Consider, for instance, the discussion of the Icelandic Fascist Party, a party that at no point was ever been able to muster more than three hundred members![9] But as far as can be ascertained, no academic specialising in the field has ever regarded Plaid Cymru as having been a Fascist party in any respect whatsoever.[10]

A further obvious possibility to consider is Plaid Cymru's own attitude towards Fascism. Has the party at any time ever regarded itself as a Fascist party, or supposed that it shared common ground with Fascism?

The party leadership actually paid very little attention to the rise of Fascism. The only exception is a somewhat confused comment by Ambrose Bebb made before the founding of party in 1924, that managed to praise Fascist Mussolini and Communist Lenin in the same breath, each for resisting what he regarded as the tepid parliamentarianism of his day.[11] It was only in 1934, a year after Hitler had assumed power in Germany, that the party give serious consideration to its position on Fascism. That was a particularly significant year in the history of Fascism in Britain, and it should come as no surprise that this was when Plaid Cymru set out its position clearly and unequivocally. The first months of 1934 saw Oswald Mosley's British Union of Fascists reach its high-water mark.[12] With the enthusiastic support of Lord Rothermere, owner of *The Daily Mail*, and further bolstered by sympathy from other elements within the British establishment, the BUF and its Blackshirts grew into a movement of some 50,000 members. The tide only turned against the BUF in the wake of the violent treatment meted out by Fascist stewards to their opponents at a mass BUF rally at London's Olympia, in June 1934. This was also the month of Hitler's infamous 'Night of the Long Knives' in which dozens of 'left-wing' Nazis as well as opponents of Nazism on the Authoritarian Right (a term which will be further discussed below) were murdered. This was another blow to the credibility of Fascism. By the end of 1934, Fascism appears to have lost most of its appeal for the British electorate.

The first significant statement on Fascism by the Plaid Cymru leadership was made in a speech delivered by Saunders Lewis at a party-organised 'Noson Lawen' social event in Cardiff to celebrate St David's Day 1934, and reported by the *Western Mail*. According to Lewis,

> It was probable that there would be a successful Fascist movement in Britain which would be vigorously opposed to Welsh Nationalism. In the Fascist's Totalitarian State freedom for Wales would be an impossibility.
> 'It is possible,' he added, 'that there would be bloodshed in South Wales if there is a Fascist Government. In such a case the Nationalist

Party must take sides with the popular masses of Wales against Fascist dictatorship.'[13]

This is a striking statement that has not been given the attention it deserves. At a time when Fascism was riding high in Britain, here was Saunders Lewis making crystal clear that Plaid Cymru would stand alongside – indeed the clear implication is that it would *fight* alongside – the working class in Wales ('the popular masses') against the Fascists should they ever assume power.

In his editorial notes for the July issue of *Y Ddraig Goch*, Saunders Lewis provided a more complete statement of Plaid Cymru's position.[14] 'Fear, oppression and cruelty are not the only characteristics of Fascism. As a political teaching, it also contains within it qualities that are to be admired'. Such admiration was due, it seems, to the extent that Fascism turned for inspiration to 'the best traditions of a pre-capitalist and pre-industrial Europe'. However, Lewis went on, 'the Nationalist Party must declare its opposition to Fascism, even, indeed, if we were to witness such a phenomenon as Welsh Fascism'. The basis for this opposition was the Fascist idealisation of the state: 'For Fascists, the State is sacrosanct, and the rights of the State are given supremacy in the lives of its subjects.' This was not only contrary to Plaid Cymru's fundamental political and philosophical emphasis on the need to devolve both political power and capital as widely as possible; it was also a belief that carried with it very dangerous implications:

> [T]he growth of Fascism endangers world peace through its glorification of a dictatorial and unconditional [*diamod*] state. A country subject to Fascist order will be marshalled as an army, and will become in and of itself a war machine. Its government will assume the form of a General [*Cadfridog*], or of a Communist government.[14]

Were Fascism ever to assume power in England, then 'Woe betide Wales . . . and woe betide her unemployed and unprotected people.' The only possible resistance in such a situation would be 'a united Wales maintaining the rights of a nation'. In the face of the Fascist threat, therefore, 'we plead with the industrial workers and the workers of Wales to join us in the Welsh Nationalist Party, before it is too late.'

From this point on, there were frequent references to Fascism in Plaid Cymru periodicals. So, for example, like so many of his contemporaries, whilst under no illusions about the 'the false philosophy of the Nazis', J. E. Daniel found that there were lessons that could be learned from individual policy programmes – in his case, it was the Nazis' agricultural policy.[15] In addition, the party was increasingly required to defend itself against accusations that it was somehow Fascist in orientation – hence R. E. Jones's essay in the November 1934 issue of *Y Ddraig Goch*, 'Are we Fascists? God forbid!' But fundamentally the party's position did not shift in any fundamental way from that set out in the first half of 1934. Plaid Cymru opposed Fascism and, indeed, considered Fascism to be an enemy of the values represented by Welsh nationalism. This does not amount to claiming that Plaid Cymru was beyond reproach in terms of the reception it gave to Fascism. Those on the party's right wing were more prone to lapses in judgement than others – which was, of course, entirely typical of the historical conjuncture. Specifically, Ambrose Bebb wrote an essay on Mussolini for *Y Ddraig Goch* in August 1935 in which, courtesy of his characteristically ebullient and florid prose style, he plunged straight into deep and dangerous waters. One wonders, indeed, whether the more mature Bebb might have considered his reference to Isaiah when describing Mussolini as a man who carried 'the cross of his nation raised high', to be verging on the blasphemous. Nevertheless, while arguing that Mussolini's attack invasion of Abyssinia was an attempt to civilise that country, Bebb also conceded that this 'did not legitimise waging war against her, and her destruction and ruin'.[16]

A close reading of Saunders Lewis's writing from the 1930s in search of evidence of his alleged Fascist proclivities discloses that, beyond an interest in particular policy programmes – which, as previously noted, was quite typical of the period among those seeking policy responses adequate to the challenge of the Great Depression – Lewis makes two observations that might be construed as praise for two of the period's lesser-known Fascist leaders, Léon

Degrelle and Jacques Doriot.[17] Degrelle was the leader of the Rex movement in Belgium, and Doriot – a former member of the central committee of the French Communist Party – was the founder of the new Parti Populaire Français (PPF).[18] Lewis's comments appeared in the October 1936 issue of *The Welsh Nationalist*. Rex emerged as an increasingly Fascist movement after 1937, aiding the Nazis after Germany's occupation of Belgium in 1940. Despite the fact that its leader and many of its members came from a left-wing background, the PPF moved quickly to the right following the party's founding, shortly after the general election held in France in May 1936. And, in the wake of the German occupation of France, Doriot became a staunch supporter of the occupiers. In fairness to Saunders Lewis, therefore, neither Degrelle nor Doriot were Fascists at the time that he wrote in their praise. What is important for the present discussion, however, is that his praise for them stemmed from their perceived support for 'widely-divided private property': 'This is something entirely different from that State-Capitalism which is the hallmark alike of the Nazi, Fascist and Communist state'.[19] Leaving aside whether Lewis's categorisation was accurate – and as the first PPF conference was only held in November 1936, Lewis was unlikely to have had much detailed knowledge about what the PPF actually stood for – his positive remarks were premised on the assumption that Degrelle and Doriot were *not* Fascists. As such, Lewis remained consistent in his views.[20]

3

Defining Fascism

At no time did the Plaid Cymru leadership consider the party to be a Fascist party. Indeed, its opposition to Fascism was consistent and unequivocal even *before* Fascism was finally rendered beyond the pale. It is also evident that Fascist parties saw no common ground between themselves and Welsh nationalism. Additionally, nowhere in the vast corpus of academic literature on Fascism do we find any discussion of Plaid Cymru as a Fascist party or a party that had any meaningful association with Fascism. Of course, we must consider the possibility that they were all mistaken: that the members and leadership of Plaid Cymru failed to understand the real nature of their own views; that 'true' Fascists failed to recognise this existence of a sister-organisation in Wales; and that later academics have similarly failed to note the Fascist underbelly of Welsh nationalism. All of this is extremely unlikely, to say the very least. Yet, as the accusations made against Plaid Cymru came from Welshmen of real standing and status, we must take the possibility seriously. That in turn means that must enter the quagmire that awaits anyone seeking to define Fascism.

As has already been made clear, there is no consensus as to what Fascism was or is. Different commentators identify different elements and aspects of Fascism as its primary features.[1] Roger Griffin, for example, attempts a concise definition of Fascism based on the Fascist emphasis on national rebirth through the force of populist, extreme nationalism.[2] In Griffin's view, the essence of Fascism is that it is a 'palingenetic form of populist ultra-nationalism'. By contrast, Michael Mann argues – correctly, in my view – that national rebirth is a common characteristic of all nationalism rather than of Fascism per se. Mann's alternative definition of Fascism is that it is 'the pursuit of a transcendent and cleansing nation-statism through paramilitarism'.[3] Through this definition, Mann seeks to underscore the Fascist belief that, through rigid control of society, a strong state can transcend or even eradicate social divisions (be they class or ethnic divisions), creating a new form of society that is unified and 'pure'. The reference to paramilitarism focuses attention on one of Fascism's main characteristics, namely its glorification of violence and military organisation as a means of transforming society. In Mann's words, 'Fascism was always uniformed, marching, armed, dangerous, and radically destabilizing of the existing order.'[4]

Stanley Payne's contribution to this area of study is considered as among the most important, with his *A History of Fascism 1914–45* widely acknowledged as a classic work. Payne offers no definition of Fascism as such, but rather opts for a 'descriptive typology' that allows for a comparative study of Fascism's varied forms and expressions. A host of elements is drawn into this typology. These include negative elements; that is ideologies to which Fascists declared their opposition: they were anti-Liberal, anti-Communist and anti-Conservative. Payne also draws attention to the 'style and organisation' of Fascism with its emphasis on militarism, mysticism, masculinity, youth and charismatic, dictatorial leadership. He further emphasises the importance of the following features of Fascist political programmes: the desire to build an authoritarian state on entirely new foundations (rather than on traditional principles); imperialism; a belief that class divisions can be overcome by corporate or syndicalist social organisation; and a belief in the positive, cleansing role of violence and war.[5]

Payne insists that distinctions must be drawn between the various right-wing authoritarian movements that emerged in interwar Europe. Though these movements may have had common enemies in Marxism and Liberalism, their differences were actually so fundamental that arbitrarily to label all of them 'fascist' is as misleading as 'identifying Stalinism and Rooseveltian democracy because both were opposed to Hitlerism, Japanese militarism, and western European colonialism'.[6] Specifically, Payne seeks to distinguish between the Conservative Right, the Radical Right and Fascism. He bases this typology on important ideological differences: in comparison with Fascism, the Conservative Right was more right-wing and more conservative. Despite rejecting the commitment of other Conservatives to operating within the framework of democratic constitutionalism, the Conservative Right nonetheless stressed such familiar Conservative themes as Order and Tradition. They also accorded a central social role to religion. All of this was in contrast to the Fascist emphasis on the need for revolutionary action that would allow society to be rebuilt on entirely new foundations; foundations that would, for all practical purposes, completely marginalise traditional religion.

Payne positions the Radical Right somewhere between the Fascists and the Conservative Right:

> If fascists and conservative authoritarians often stood at nearly opposite poles culturally and philosophically, various elements of the radical right tended to span the entire spectrum. Some radical groups, as in Spain, were just as conservative culturally and as formally religious as was the conservative authoritarian right. Others, primarily in central Europe, tended increasingly to embrace vitalist and biological doctrines not significantly different from those of core fascists. Still others, in France and elsewhere, adopted a rigidly rationalistic position quite different from the nonrationalism and vitalism of the fascists, while trying to adopt in a merely formalistic guise a political framework of religiosity.[7]

As well as marking these ideological distinctions, Payne also notes the complexity of the relationships that existed between Fascists, the Radical Right and Authoritarian Conservatives: at certain times and in certain places, they could collaborate; at other times, they could be enemies (even mortal enemies), especially so the Authoritarian Right and Fascists.

FORMS OF AUTHORITARIAN CONSERVATISM
[PAYNE'S TABLE MODIFIED]

	FASCISTS	THE RADICAL RIGHT	THE CONSERVATIVE RIGHT
Germany	NSDAP	Hugenburg, Papen, Stahlhelm	Hindenburg, Brüning, Schleicher
Italy	PNF	ANI	Sonnino, Salandra
Belgium	Rex (late), Verdinaso, Légion Nationale		Rex (early), VNV
France	Francistes, PPF, RNP	Action Française, Jeunesses Patriotes, Solidarité Française	Croix de Feu, Vichy
Spain	Falange	Carlists, Renovación Española	CEDA

Robert O. Paxton agrees in large measure with Payne's arguments and in particular with his insistence on the importance of distinguishing between Fascism and other manifestations of right-wing, authoritarian politics.[8] He emphasises the Fascist desire to impose complete state control on the private lives of state subjects; this is in contrast to the way in which Conservatives (be they of authoritarian or democratic sensibilities) acknowledge the importance and autonomy of the various social spheres that mediate between the state and the individual – the family, religious organisations, the military, etc. Discussing the difference between Fascism and varied types of Authoritarian Conservatism, Paxton draws attention to the fact that:

> Authoritarians would rather leave the population demobilized and passive, while fascists want to engage and excite the public. Authoritarians want a strong but limited state. They hesitate to intervene in the economy, as fascism does readily, or to embark on programs of social welfare. They cling to the status quo rather than proclaim a new way.[9]

Turning to the difference between Fascism and Conservatism more generally, Paxton's position has been summarised in characteristically eloquent style by the Marxist literary critic Terry Eagleton:

> Conservatives believe in God, tradition, the monarchy, civilisation and the individual, whereas fascists are pagan, primitivist, collectivist state-worshippers who prefer jackboots to crowns ... Fascists admire productive workers (including productive capitalists) and denounce effete aristocrats and the idle rich; conservatives tend to champion both groups, among whose ranks they themselves can frequently be found ... Fascists strut, while conservatives lounge ... Conservatives disdain the popular masses, while fascists mobilise and manipulate them. Some conservatives believe in ideas, but fascists have a marked preference for myths. If they think at all, they think through their blood, not their brain. Fascists regard themselves as a youthful, revolutionary avant-garde out to erase the botched past and create an unimaginable new future.[10]

Fascists are radicals, whose goal is entirely to transform society and to create a new man to live within it. In contrast, a respect for continuity and tradition is the common ground upon which the many forms of Conservatism converge.

Whilst in many ways illuminating and suggestive, the quest for an agreed-upon definition of Fascism is almost certainly doomed to failure. Yet, to study the relevant literature is to be struck by the way in which certain features are invariably associated with Fascism. These are:

- the glorification of the state;
- the glorification of violence; and,
- the glorification of the leader and leadership (the infamous *Führerprinzip*).

The presence of each is not enough in itself to allow us to declare without equivocation that we are in the presence of Fascism. We may encounter other groups and organisations that cleave to and privilege one or two – or perhaps even all three – of these features. But what can be said with some certainty is that their absence signals that 'Fascist' is not at all the appropriate designation for the object of study. The next step, therefore, will be to consider each in the context of Plaid Cymru. It is also appropriate that we consider anti-Semitism. Whilst anti-Semitism may not counted as one of the fundamental characterstics of Fascism, the alleged anti-Semitism of Plaid Cymru (or at least of some of the party's most prominent members) has featured in some of the most recent accusations of Fascist tendencies made against it.

The state

The position of Fascists in relation to the state is summed up in one of the slogans of Mussolini and his followers: *Tutto nello Stato, neinte al di fuori Stato, nulla contro lo Stato*. Everything in the state, nothing outside the state, nothing against the state. Fascists privileged, glorified and even worshipped the state. Their aim was to make everything that took place within the state – every aspect of public and private life – subject to the will and rule of the state. It is true to say that no Fascist state ever achieved its ideal in this regard. Such was the social authority of Roman Catholicism in Italy, for instance, that Mussolini had to extend it considerable privileges via the 1929 Lateran Treaty. Even in Nazi Germany, recent historiography has emphasised how chaotic and divided the state actually was in terms of its internal organisation. But whatever the reality, in principle at least, totalitarianism was the goal for Fascists. By means of the omnipotent state, man and society could be created anew in the ideal image of Fascism.

It is hard to imagine a more inappropriate accusation to level against Plaid Cymru than state idolatry. Such a notion runs directly counter to the party's consistent emphasis on the importance of diffusing power as widely as possible throughout society, rather than concentrating it in the hands of the centralised state. Suspicion of the over-centralised and omnipotent state was in fact the common denominator between D. J. Davies's emphasis on decentralisation and cooperation and Saunders Lewis's *perchentyaeth*.[11] Indeed, so implacable was Lewis's suspicion that he even opposed state provision of medical services to schoolchildren in Wales during the Depression on the basis that this would usurp the proper role of the family.[12] If there is a criticism to be made of Saunders Lewis's views of the state, it is that his abhorrence of totalitarianism led him greatly to *underestimate* the progressive role that can played by state provision.[13]

It should come as no surprise, therefore, that the party's consistent opposition to the centralised totalitarian state was one of the key planks of Plaid Cymru's defence against the accusations of Fascism with which it was confronted. Here is J. E. Daniel's response to Gwilym Davies's claim that Plaid Cymru would foster totalitarianism:

> Is Mr Davies going to risk his reputation as a student of politics and an honest man by claiming that this is the doctrine of the Welsh Nationalist Party? Has he not read *Why we burnt the Bombing School?* There he will find that three Christians, one Catholic, one Baptist, the other a Calvinistic Methodist, went to Wormwood Scrubs prison, as protest against not only the totalitarian claims of the English state but also the totalitarian outlook as a whole. Has he not read that the basis of our agricultural policy is the co-operative smallholding, and that we aim for the decentralisation of industry, the workers having a voice in its direction? How can totalitarianism agree with this? Does Mr Davies seriously think that we desire to free Wales from the stranglehold of English totalitarianism in order to facilitate a surrender to Welsh totalitarianism? . . . It is an unpardonable lie to suggest that the Welsh Nationalist Party wishes to do what the Communists have done in Russia and the Nazis in Germany.[14]

We shall in due course return to the appropriateness – and the consequences – of this tendency to conflate 'English totalitarianism' with Stalin's Soviet Union and Hitler's Germany. In the meantime, however, let us simply concede that the party and its leadership was consistent and sincere in its opposition to totalitarianism. Far from glorifying the institution of the state, throughout its history Plaid Cymru has tended to regard the state with suspicion.

The glorification of violence

Fascists were not the first to glorify violence or to believe that conflict, and militarism more generally, could be a beneficial, even providential, force. Before the carnage of the First World War began to bring civilised nations to their senses, the glorification of violence was evident right across the political spectrum. Consider, for instance, the emphasis placed by Georges Sorel and so many of his fellow Syndicalists on direct, violent action as a means of not only transforming society, but also (via the very act itself) of conferring dignity upon workers. Indeed, even after the catastrophe of the trenches, uniformed, militia-type organisations were a typical feature of European political parties throughout the 1920s and 1930s.[15] The belief that the type of discipline instilled by drilling, uniforms and so on, should be celebrated and encouraged, was so commonplace as to assume the status of common sense. Witness Baden-Powell's Boy Scouts, or even Ifan ab Owen Edwards's Urdd youth movement in Wales.

There was, nevertheless, something terrifyingly unique about the extent to which Fascism fetishised violence and militarism. Paramilitarism was central to its internal organisation and external appearance, and extreme violence a key means of bending society to its will – generating unity by targeting scapegoats and suppressing dissent. But Fascists not only glorified violence as a means to an end: they further believed that that it contained within itself a dignity and even a beauty. For Fascists, violence assumed what might be termed an aesthetic quality. And because they deferred to no moral compass beyond their own – or that of the state once they had assumed control of it – there was no 'in principle' reason why their violence should be moderated. Believing that the strongest would inevitably triumph, the violence of the Fascist party and state signalled the superiority of their virile masculinity over the tired and degenerate old world that they were in the process of displacing.

It is impossible to be certain what proportion of the members of the interwar Welsh Nationalist Party were pacifists. But pacifism became a mainstay of Welsh Nonconformity during its dying days as a significant social force and, with conscientious Welsh Nonconformists playing such a central role in the life of the party, that proportion would undoubtedly have been very high. Needless to say, this group abhorred rather than glorified violence. Even among those Welsh nationalists who rejected pacifism as an absolute principle, there was none of the romanticisation of violence that had characterised Irish nationalism, for example, not to mention Fascist glorifications of violence. Saunders Lewis may have spoken of 'drilling' Welsh nationalists in a speech that he made before the founding of Plaid Cymru, but he dismissed H. R. Jones's 'Sinn Féin-ism' in 1925, and in 1934 rejected outright any idea of drilling party members. Moreover, while the need for 'sacrifice' [aberth] was a standard rhetorical trope of Welsh nationalism from the founding days of Plaid Cymru, its aim was to inspire self-sacrifice and not the blood sacrifice of Pádraig Pearse. In short, there are simply no grounds for believing that Plaid Cymru, or any individual of any prominence within the party, ever glorified violence.

The glorification of leaders and leadership

One of the most striking characteristics of Fascists and Fascism is the tendency to glorify a charismatic leader. In the words of Stanley Payne, 'all fascist movements came to espouse variants of a *Führerprinzip*'.[16]

The Fascist leader claimed a mystical connection to his people. This was a direct, emotional bond that could not be explained by mere reason alone and that certainly should never be constrained by traditional constitutional convention. This connection could allow the Fascist leader to elevate his people to

> a higher realm of politics that they would experience sensually: the warmth of belonging to a race now fully aware of its identity, historic destiny, and power; the excitement of participating in a vast collective enterprise; the gratification of submerging oneself in a wave of shared feelings, and of sacrificing one's petty concerns for the group's good; and the thrill of domination.[17]

As a consequence of this ability to foresee the destiny of a people and to secure its fulfilment, the Fascist leader could demand absolute submission and obedience. After all, he (and they were all men, reflecting Fascism's phallocentricism) was the font of all authority. If Fascism is a secular religion, as many commentators have claimed, then the Fascist leader is a Messianic figure – to be exalted, worshipped and obeyed without question.

We have already seen how some claimed to identify commonalities between Saunders Lewis's role within the Welsh Nationalist Party and Hitler's within the Nazi Party. For students of Lewis's life and work – or the history of the first two decades of the party over which he presided – this comparison is so laughably inappropriate that it is very hard to believe that those who suggested it ever expected it to be taken seriously. We can be confident that Saunders Lewis never imagined that he enjoyed some mystical bond with the people of Wales. Indeed, it is his 'elitist' distance and alienation from the lives of the vast majority of the population that has tended to incur the censure of most of his critics. Even if there was always an element of exaggeration in this charge – Lewis experienced more of the vicissitudes and hardships of life than the vast majority of those who have sought to castigate him – we can surely agree that populism or the 'common touch' were not his *forte*. In his famous Freudian dissection of Fascist propaganda, Theodor Adorno described how essential it was for the Fascist leader to

> still resemble the follower and appear as his 'enlargement'. Accordingly, one of the devices of personalized fascist propaganda is the concept of the 'great little man', a person who suggests both omnipotence and the idea that he is just one of the folks.[18]

Who could ever have imagined the aristocratic Saunders Lewis as 'one of the folks'? He himself certainly didn't. And to the extent that the president of the Welsh Nationalist Party could be considered a 'great little man', then it would be as a literal description of his diminutive stature and formidable intellectual capabilities, rather than as an exercise in Freudian conceptualisation.

Even in terms of Plaid Cymru's internal politics, Saunders Lewis was far from being a dictator. True, he did insist on having his own way on certain programmatic points during the founding of the party.[19] It is also undeniable that Lewis and his leadership were viewed with the utmost respect by most (though not all) of the party faithful. There were some among them who might even be said to have idolised him. Yet the party conference was its sovereign body; that is where party policy was ultimately decided. And on at least two occasions during his career as president of Plaid Cymru, the party conference passed key motions to which Lewis was fiercely opposed – one on ending its policy of absententionism with regards Westminster, the other on the issue of pacifism.[20] On both occasions, he accepted the party's decision. J. E. Daniel was correct when he stated that 'The conference of the Nationalist Party, representing its branches, is its ultimate authority of the Party. There is no place in its constitution for the *Führerprinzip*.'[21] He might even have gone further. The fact of the matter is that criticism – often, trenchant criticism – of various aspects of Plaid Cymru's policy programme was a regular feature of the party's periodical publications throughout Lewis's alleged 'Hitlerian' presidency. The claim that there was some kind of common ground between the role of the Fascist leader and the role of Saunders Lewis in the life of Plaid Cymru is utterly unsustainable.

Anti-Semitism

Anti-Semitism and Fascism have become synonymous. This should come as no surprise given the quite catastrophic human consequences of the Nazis' pathological anti-Semitism. The historical reality is, however, far more complex. On the one hand, murderous anti-Semitism was not confined to the ranks of the Nazi Party alone. It has been a scourge on Western 'civilisation' over many long centuries. On the other hand, a rather lesser-known fact is that during the first sixteen years of Mussolini's reign, Italian Fascism adopted a quite different position in relation to the Jews than the one assumed by the Nazis in Germany. In Italy, Jews were prominent among Il Duce's active supporters and financial backers. Indeed, it has been estimated that some two hundred Jews joined the March on Rome that carried the Fascists to power. Jews featured also among the leader's friends and even lovers.[22] Before 1938, when anti-Jewish legislation was implemented in Italy as Mussolini moved to throw in his lot definitively with Hitler, one in every three Italian Jews was a member of the Fascist party.[23] Yet, although anti-Semitism cannot be counted as being one of the fundamental characteristics of Fascism, it is by now clearly an important part of what is being invoked when the term 'Fascist' is deployed. As such, it is appropriate that we consider whether or not anti-Semitism was a feature of the political philosophy, policy programme or rhetorical armoury of Plaid Cymru.[24]

Saunders Lewis's alleged anti-Semitism has received considerable attention following the publication of D. Tecwyn Lloyd's biography in 1988.[25] A close reading of Lewis's writings certainly throws up a number of comments relating to the Jews that reveal what Meredydd Evans has termed 'crude ethnic prejudices' (*rhagfarnau cenhedlig amrwd*). The best known example is undoubtedly Lewis's poem 'Y Dilyw 1939' (The Deluge 1939), with its reference to the 'Hebrew nostrils' of the 'gods' of Wall Street – it may indeed be the only such example in the entire corpus of his creative writing.[26] Similar comments can be found in his political essays. So, for example, one of the topics he discusses in the December 1926 issue of *Y Ddraig Goch*, is the role played by Jews in both international capitalism and Communism. Lewis cites Sir Alfred Mond, the famous industrialist and MP for Carmarthen, alongside Karl Marx as two examples of 'napoleonic Jews' who have 'shaped the economic ideas of the modern world'.[27] In Mond's case, his lack of roots in or adherence to the Christian tradition meant that he was indifferent to 'the destruction of the spiritual heritage of England and Wales and

Ireland' that was the consequence of 'tearing Britain away from Europe, and dividing the world up into three economic armies, Europe, America, the British empire'. 'Power and authority' were his only concerns.[28]

In an essay published in the June 1933 issue of *Y Ddraig Goch* discussing the power of the English press in forming public opinion, Lewis made reference to the influence of Jews on the London press. He wondered, in particular, at the dramatic change in journalistic attitudes towards Germany that had recently taken place: in a relatively short period of time, broad support had been replaced by unanimous condemnation. The supposed reason for this *volte face* was outrage at the persecution of German Jews. But as this treatment was only the fulfilment of Hitler's long broadcast intentions, Lewis judged this to be insufficient explanation. Rather, his suggestion was that Jewish financial influence had secured this change in opinion along Fleet Street.[29]

In addition to these comments, Lewis wrote an essay discussing small-scale capitalism, which argued – inter alia – for legislation prohibiting the accumulation of property and wealth in the hands of powerful capitalists – legislation that would be powerful enough to give pause to 'even the Jews of Bangor'.[30] In a speech delivered in the build-up to the burning at Penyberth, Lewis spoke of the contribution of bankers' 'usury' in fomenting international wars – the kind of language frequently associated with anti-Semitism.[31]

For some of his critics, such comments are further evidence of Saunders Lewis's Fascist proclivities – or at least of his Fascist sympathies. Tecwyn Lloyd claims that 'there is only a difference in degree between such things and the repulsive madness of Julius Streicher in his *Der Stürmer* during the Third Reich'.[32] The reality, however, is more prosaic – and in many ways less reassuring. The few anti-Semitic references found in Lewis's writings are a reflection of the way in which crude ethnic prejudices, and anti-Semitism in particular, were part of the cultural currency of the era; and while Tecwyn Lloyd might have us believe that Lewis was an external influence defiling the radical purity of traditional Welsh-speaking Wales, such crude ethnic prejudices were as prevalent in Wales as they were on the other side of Offa's Dyke.[33]

To attempt to list every prominent figure in British life during the first half of the twentieth century who made anti-Semitic remarks would be a hugely laborious and deeply depressing task. For instance, as well as praising Mussolini, Winston Churchill, the nemesis of Fascism in so many respects, was also the author of an essay arguing that the Bolshevik Revolution was the creation of rootless, 'international Jews'. Churchill described their role in terms of a 'world-wide conspiracy for the overthrow of civilization and for the reconstitution of society on the basis of arrested development, of envious malevolence, and impossible equality'. This alleged conspiracy had been the 'mainspring of every subversive movement' since the nineteenth century.[34] Such prejudices were common. Indeed, discussing English literature, George Orwell once argued that there could easily be identified

> a perceptible antisemitic strain in English literature from Chaucer onwards, and without even getting up from this table to consult a book I can think of passages which IF WRITTEN NOW would be stigmatised as antisemitism, in the works of Shakespeare, Smollett, Thackeray, Bernard Shaw, H. G. Wells, T. S. Eliot, Aldous Huxley and various others. Offhand, the only English writers I can think of who, before the days of Hitler, made a definite effort to stick up for Jews are Dickens and Charles Reade.[35]

The great irony is that Orwell's own writings feature anti-Semitic remarks: among them the complaint that the London press was controlled by Jews.[36]

Anti-Semitism could be found throughout Europe and right across the political spectrum in Britain; from George Orwell and H. G. Wells on the left to Churchill and T. S. Eliot on the right. In Wales, Lloyd George managed to combine what is sometimes termed *philo*-Semitism – respect for the great contribution made by Jews and, in Lloyd George's case, enthusiastic support for the creation of a Jewish homeland – with the casual anti-Semitism so typical of his time.[37] Even more striking in the context of the present discussion are the anti-Semitic utterances of that self-proclaimed advocate of 'Reason and Freedom', W. J. Gruffydd. In his editorial notes for Y *Llenor* in the Spring of 1941 (written, therefore, during the darkest days of the Second World War), Gruffydd complained that 'North Wales is full of wealthy, scheming Jews who arrogate to themselves all the resources of the land leaving the native population helpless and impoverished'. He went on:

> And by the way, is it not high time that somebody protested loudly against those Jews who oppress Llandudno, Colwyn Bay, Abergele and the surrounding countryside? Are the Jews utterly unable to learn from the history of their nation [*cenedl*] in other lands? . . . They have yet to realise that they have absolved all responsibility for the dire condition of their nation in the Nazi states. It appears to me that they have two, and only two, primary objectives – to flee from danger wherever they may be, regardless of the dangers that others may face; and to pursue their traditional method of enriching themselves at the expense of gentiles. 'Antisemitism,' you say. Not at all. Rather, a timely word of warning for a nation which deserves the best that the world can offer, but which faces a real threat in this country as in every other country after the war if they continue to conduct themselves in their present manner. If this warning is ignored, they shall become a problem in Wales as well as in England, and when a nation becomes a problem, it cannot expect justice and fairness from a population that suffers because of it. The pity is that such a warning can only be sounded in an unassuming quarterly such as *Y Llenor*, of which the great wide world knows nothing. And the reason for this is simple – few newspapers apart from Welsh-language papers are free from the direct or indirect influence of the Jews.[38]

Rootless, selfish Jews indifferent to the destruction of tradition as they exploit others; Jewish control of the popular press: yes, all the familiar characteristics of the 'crude ethnic prejudice' are present.

Unfortunately, there is nothing particularly unusual about the few observations in Saunders Lewis's writing that can be construed as anti-Semitic. In fact, it would appear that he was more aware than most of the ugliness of such sentiment. Alongside his observations on Sir Alfred Mond, he concedes how 'It is a poor and servile (*gwael a thaeogaidd*) thing to try to besmirch a man by calling him a Jew'.[39] When Lewis spoke of the part that Jewish influence had played in altering the prevailing view about Nazism in the London press, he also acknowledged that innocent Jews were being unfairly persecuted.[40] In 1938, he warned again against the 'anti-Semitism that is one of history's diseases and that can take hold in all of us if given the opportunity'.[41] This is Lewis at his most perceptive; frankly admitting a temptation to which he was to surrender on more than one occasion.

The crucial point that must be emphasised, however, is that Lewis's anti-Semitism was neither a fundamental nor substantial part of his worldview – no more than was the anti-Semitism of Orwell or Churchill fundamental or substantial to theirs. Indeed, the category of race plays no part in Saunders Lewis's political thought. This does not diminish the odiousness of the sentiments to which he and a multitude of others across the political spectrum gave voice. Nonetheless, there is clearly a world of difference between this 'casual' anti-Semitism so typical of the years leading up to the Second World War, and the anti-Semitism of *Der Stürmer* and Streicher, for instance.[42] As anyone who has read his articles and speeches must surely recognise – and it is hard to believe that Tecwyn Lloyd had ever done so if he seriously believed that it was appropriate to equate them with Lewis's remarks – Streicher's anti-Semitism was systematic and utterly obsessive.[43] Nazis such as Streicher viewed the world in racialised, racist terms: it was central to their worldview. Their (perverted) moral perspective was also based on racial categories.

Finally, it should be noted that there is no hint of anti-Semitism in the Welsh Nationalist Party's political programme. When we do encounter anti-Semitic comments or pronouncements from party supporters – and contrary to the claims of certain critics, there are very, very few – they reflect 'crude ethnic prejudice' of the kind that we have identified in the writings of Saunders Lewis. There is certainly no evidence to suggest that anyone in the ranks embraced anti-Semitism as part of a systematic worldview.[44] Even in the case of Ambrose Bebb, a man deeply influenced by thinkers who were thoroughly anti-Semitic (*L'Action Française* and Maurras), his great error was that he ignored this dimension to their ideas, not that he embraced it himself.[45] In a word, Plaid Cymru was not anti-Semitic, even if some of its members and leaders failed to escape completely from the anti-Semitic undercurrent that was so much a part of the era's culture.

Measuring Plaid Cymru against the criteria established earlier in this discussion, it is evident that there was not the slightest trace of Fascism in its programme or general attitudes and, indeed, that the party actually adopted the polar opposite position to Fascists on all of these essential criteria. Rather than glorifying the state, Plaid Cymru was extremely cautious of the state's encroaching influence; rather than glorifying violence, the party inclined towards pacifism; and, though the party's rank and file may have viewed Saunders Lewis and Gwynfor Evans after him with the greatest respect, the kind of glorification of a leader (and of leadership as a general principle) that characterised Fascism was anathema to them. Not only was this not a Fascist programme; neither was there anything that could have been remotely described as Fascist in the attitudes of party members. As Prosser Rhys pointed out at the time, the vast majority of the party rank and file tended towards the left of the political spectrum, and so too the party leadership after the Second World War. Before and during the war, it is indeed true that some right-wingers played very prominent roles at the head of the party, but, again, they were not Fascists. They did not even belong to the Conservative Right, as Payne would define it. Rather, as Saunders Lewis admitted of himself, he was a conservative. Granted, his form of conservatism was to become increasingly rare during the twentieth century: this was a romantic conservatism that recoiled from the effects of industrial capitalism on traditional society, while at the same time fostering bold and progressive cultural experimentation. An idiosyncratic and inconsistent conservatism in the eyes of many, perhaps, yet an acknowledged form of conservatism nonetheless. Ambrose Bebb was also a conservative, even if he was enamoured of certain aspects of the Radical Right's worldview in the shape of *L'Action Française*.

On the issue of anti-Semitism, some members of Plaid Cymru were not entirely free from those reprehensible prejudices that were typical of the time. But instances of anti-Semitism in party literature are very rare, and are counterbalanced by eloquent condemnations of such prejudice. What is more, there is not a trace of anti-Semitism on the party programme.

If we take seriously the accusations of Fascism made against the party, we must conclude that there is simply no truth attached to them. Plaid Cymru was never a Fascist party, nor did it sympathise with Fascism. One central question, therefore, remains. In light of the complete absence of evidence to support the accusations, why were they ever taken seriously in the first place and why have they been repeated subsequently with such apparent conviction? The following response to these questions is in two parts: the first concerns the attitude adopted by the party towards the Spanish Civil War and the Second World War; the second concerns the nature of Welsh political culture more generally.

4

Wales During a Decade of War

The decade from the mid-1930s to the mid-1940s proved to be the most bloody in human history. Mussolini's forces attacked Abyssinia in October 1935; July 1936 saw the start of the Spanish Civil War; Italy attacked Albania in April 1939; while in the same period in the Far East, China endured a war between the Communists, Chiang Kai-Shek's Nationalists, the Japanese, and a host of minor warlords, with the Japanese also launching a number of military excursions into the Soviet Union. By September 1939, a general and truly global war was underway as the British and French empires declared war against Germany, following the latter's invasion of Poland (with the aid and cooperation of the Soviet Union). The Second World War would not end until the formal surrender of Japan in September 1945. Around fifty million lives had been lost.[1]

All of this, of course, had an enormous effect on Wales and, as a consequence, on Plaid Cymru. Specifically, the positions that the party adopted with regards to these conflicts became central to the accusations of Fascism made against it – as well as to the party's attempts to defend itself against such accusations. Bearing this in mind, it is striking the extent to which the evidence suggests that Plaid Cymru's general attitude to international relations, and to war, was broadly consistent with majority opinion in Wales in 1935 (or at least with the most vocal elements in Welsh public life). Moreover, the party's position remained extraordinarily consistent over the decade that followed. Both the party's leadership and membership held fast to a number of core beliefs, most notably that war itself was the real enemy, and that the wickedness and hypocrisy that characterised British imperialism meant that Britain could not claim the moral high ground in international affairs. Yet, while these ideas were shared in some form or another across much of the political spectrum in Wales and Britain during the mid-1930s, by the end of the decade they had come to be regarded as heretical, treasonous and 'Fascist'. Understanding Plaid Cymru's attitudes towards these ten years of horrifically bloody warfare – and how others perceived these attitudes – is vital if we are to understand the vitriolic treatment of Welsh nationalism by its enemies.

The first crucial point to note – and to be borne in mind in all of what follows – is that international relations were not high on the agenda of the Welsh Nationalist Party in the mid-1930s. The party leadership's priority was rather to discover or invent a symbolic cause around which it might evangelise; a cause that could form the focus of a campaign of national redemption capable of shaking Wales from its torpor in the run-up to the four hundredth anniversary of the Acts of Union. In 1935, such a cause emerged in the shape of the UK government's decision to build a bombing school on the Llŷn peninsula. For many years subsequently, the fate of Plaid Cymru was bound up with the events that are invoked (for Welsh speakers, at least) by the name 'Penyberth' – the initial campaigning against the establishment of a bombing school, the arson attack on the construction site, the court hearings in Caernarfon and then the Old Bailey, the imprisonment of Y Tri ('the three' – namely, Saunders Lewis, Lewis Valentine and D. J. Williams), and Lewis's subsequent dismissal by his employers at Swansea University. There were undoubtedly international elements to the party's stand on the proposed bombing school. The three protagonists described their stand as a rejection of war, militarism and totalitarianism. There can be no doubt, however, that their primary concerns centred on Wales, Welsh identity, and the future of the Welsh language.

With so much of the energies of this still small and poorly resourced party focused on 'Penyberth', comparatively little attention was paid in party literature to the burning international issue of the day, namely the Spanish Civil War.[2] Nonetheless that war has played a central part in creating the myth of Plaid Cymru as a Fascist party.

It was the Spanish Civil War that created in Wales the tendency to conflate Catholicism and Fascism, a conflation that featured so prominently in the subsequent attacks on Plaid Cymru. As Robert Stradling demonstrates in his important book *Wales and the Spanish Civil War: The Dragon's Dearest Cause?*, this crude conflation became a standard rhetorical trope for the supporters of the Republic.[3] We should perhaps not be overly surprised at this development. The Catholic Church did, after all, ally itself with the military opponents of the Republic, and Franco's rebel forces did receive considerable aid from the Fascist states.[4] From the perspective of a country like Wales where fierce anti-Catholic prejudices were deeply rooted, it was easy to believe that Roman Catholicism = Franco = Mussolini = Hitler. Contemporary historians would (at the very least) qualify each individual step in this equation; indeed, a majority would entirely refute at least some of them. So while some, for example, consider it appropriate to describe Franco as a 'Fascist' (at least up until 1942), the academic consensus seems to view him as a traditional Authoritarian Conservative who, when it suited him to do so, was temporarily and opportunistically willing to clothe his actions and beliefs in Fascist garb.[5] But during the horror and confusion of the Civil War itself, and in the context of the strong emotions it (understandably) engendered in many outside observers, few at the time were prepared to listen to those who sought to make more objective sense of it all.

Another key point to emphasise is that the Spanish Civil War now occupies a central place in one of the constitutive myths of twentieth-century Welsh politics: the myth of a Welsh working class, radical in its sensibilities and international in its outlook. The characteristic discourse surrounding this myth locates 'Spain' as the site of the first battle in the great war against Fascism, and confers a particular place of honour in that battle to the people of Wales – and of the valleys of south Wales in particular – by virtue of the participation of around one hundred and fifty Welshmen in the International Brigades. Their bravery and sacrifice stands as a monument to a cosmopolitan working class that became conscious of the part it could play – as a class – in the struggle to emancipate humanity from parochial ignorance and injustice.[6]

As with any effective myth, there is a kernel of truth here. That said, what is omitted or forgotten is as important as what is included or remembered in terms of the myth's effectiveness and productivity.[7] In this case the main omission is the fact that the situation in Spain – and the response to it in Wales – was far more complex than allowed for in the rather simplistic, black and white account that is now the received wisdom.[8] As commentators through the ages have observed, civil wars tend to be particularly cruel and barbaric. This was certainly the case in Spain, with atrocious war crimes committed on both sides. In addition, while Franco's rebellion was entirely unconstitutional, both the right and left of Spanish politics had a record of rejecting constitutional methods when it suited them to do so. Spain was a society in crisis: it was a society in which many at either end of the political spectrum rejected the state's authority unless their side held the reigns of power. There were indeed many things at stake in the Spanish Civil War, but, regrettably, liberal democracy was not one of them – especially so as the Communist Party (and therefore Moscow) assumed an increasingly prominent role in shoring up the Republic.[9]

Similarly, the response in Wales to developments in Spain was more complex than myth allows. Public opinion in Wales was far more divided than we might today imagine. Before the atrocity perpetrated by Franco and his Fascist allies against the civilian population of the Basque town of Gernika in April 1937, the daily press in Wales appears to have sympathised with the rebels rather than the Republic.[10] Even after Gernika had shifted the press's perception of what was actually happening in Spain, its sympathy and support focused in large measure on the devolved government in the Basque country rather than the Republican government itself.[11]

This ambivalence towards – and even suspicion of – the Republic was evident in the widespread support for the policy of non-intervention in the Spanish Civil War. This was the UK government's policy – a national government that included among its members both Conservatives and Liberals. Non-intervention was also the

Labour Party's policy up until October 1937, that is to say through-out the period in which intervention might have made a meaningful difference to the outcome of the conflict. Indeed, the roots of the Labour Party's Welsh organisation are (in part) grounded in the efforts of the party to counter the vigorous propaganda campaign being waged by Communists in Wales on behalf of the Republic![12] The Communist Party was the only party to have been consistent in its support for the Republic. This, of course, in a context in which that party was wholly subordinate to the interests of the Soviet Union as determined by Stalin.[13]

As with the Conservatives, the Liberals and Labour (until it was too late to make a difference), the Welsh Nationalist Party supported a policy of non-intervention. Even if we cannot be certain of the state of public attitudes at that time, it seems highly probable that the Nationalists' position also chimed with majority opinion in Wales – with the possible exception of some communities in the industrial Valleys. Indeed, when viewed in retrospect, the most striking thing about Plaid Cymru's position in relation to the Spanish Civil War is that it was not *more* different from the conventional view. After all, in Spain an alternative position was available to Plaid Cymru, and perhaps to Plaid Cymru alone. Rather than advocating non-intervention, Welsh nationalists might have called for support for the devolved governments of Catalonia and the Basque country. Such a position may well have struck a popular chord in Wales where the suffering of Basque children, in particular, had aroused considerable anger and sympathy. It would also have staked a position with obvious political resonance in a British context.

As might be expected, Plaid Cymru publications had shown a consistent interest in developments in Catalonia and the Basque country. The headline that appeared in *Y Ddraig Goch* in January 1935 sums up the tone: 'Catalonia: Y Lles a Ddeilliodd o Ymreolaeth' (Catalonia: The Benefits Deriving from Self-government).[14] Yet, despite the annual conference's expression of sympathy with the Basques in August 1937, even as the fate of the small nations that constituted part of the greater Spanish state hung in the balance, there was very much an 'arm's length' feel to the party's engagement with the Civil War. It is difficult to say with certainty what precise combination of factors accounts for this. One possibility is that, by the late 1930s, Saunders Lewis and some of his closest collaborators had become increasingly concerned by the threat of Communism and that this coloured the party's response. Absent a detailed study of Lewis's ideas, however, the extent of any shift in his views, and the relationship between those views and his party's position on Spain, remain unknown.[15] Notwithstanding Lewis's attitudes, it is also quite conceivable that the belief that the real enemy was war itself – a belief so deeply rooted in Plaid Cymru – is sufficient explanation for the party's attitude to the civil war. This was, after all, a view shared right across the Welsh Nationalist Party; by ardent pacifists as well as those like Lewis who believed that violence was sometimes necessary.

It should also be recognised that the tenor adopted in party publications towards the Spanish Civil War set the tone for the remainder of that horrific decade. Party commentators deliberately sought an analytical, objective, even dispassionate standpoint; they considered their primary purpose to be to educate rather than to agitate their readers. They sought to mitigate and moderate the strong emotions fomented by the 'English press'. As a result of this attitude, some of the alternative commentary offered up by Plaid Cymru publications proved both penetrating and perceptive. As the historian Robert Stradling has pointed out, much of the analysis of the causes of the Civil War found in contemporaneous issues of *Y Ddraig Goch* is now echoed by the current academic consensus.[16] There can be no doubt, however, that the objective, analytical tone adopted by the Welsh Nationalist leadership in relation to the conflict was a major irritant to strong supporters of the Republic – including many within the party's own ranks. When this same tone and disposition were transposed into the context of a World War that threatened the very survival of the United Kingdom itself, this irritation hardened and expanded to encompass most of the Welsh electorate, whatever their previous views on Spain.

Saunders Lewis's 'Cwrs y Byd' column in the weekly *Baner ac Amserau Cymru* proved to be Plaid Cymru's most significant public platform during the Second World War.[17] A foretaste of the column's character was given in Saunders Lewis's declaration, just days after France and Britain declared war on Germany, that 'Cwrs y Byd' would address the war 'as dispassionately and patiently as possible' (6 September 1939). On more than one occasion during the war years, Lewis had to defend himself against those who considered this attitude to be tantamount to treason:

> Our wish to be dispassionate, and to assess world leaders at a time of war dispassionately and calmly, has been misinterpreted. We are roundly condemned for not losing perspective. We are called 'barbarians' for not being suitably frenzied. We are branded 'Quislings' because we are Welsh, because we are not foolish hotheads who have been stirred up by English propaganda. (27 January 1943)

And if the tenor of this response to war was unacceptable to many, then so too was its substance. Lewis was consistent and vocal in his support for an immediate ceasefire and peace through negotiation rather than the pursuit of outright, total victory. He considered a ceasefire to be necessary for the preservation of civilisation and to be the only position consistent with Christian teaching. ('Moderating passions and nurturing tolerance are more important than calling for the aerial bombing of all of Germany and Italy' (27 January 1943).) For Lewis, a ceasefire was also the only way to guarantee that totalitarianism would not win out because, if they insisted on pursuing war until outright victory was achieved, democratic nations would find themselves adopting the Nazis' own methods of social organisation in order to defeat their enemies (5 November 1942).

All of this was controversial, to say the least. But what caused even greater consternation was another of Lewis's central contentions in support of a ceasefire. He insisted that to demand an immediate ceasefire was the only morally tenable position because both sides were jointly responsible for the war.

On occasion, Lewis's argument assumed a general, almost abstract, quality. Humanity, he believed, was essentially flawed, and so too inevitably every form of government: 'We believe that the government of Hitler is flawed,' Lewis once said, 'but that the government of Churchill is also flawed, and that it is impossible for the government of man not to be flawed' (25 March 1942). Most frequently, however, the former President of the Welsh Nationalist Party (as well as other party spokespersons) concentrated on the role played by 'England's hypocrisy' in plunging the world into the current conflict.

The double standards of the British Empire and of its supporters in Wales were a long-standing and familiar theme in the speeches and writings of Welsh nationalists. As the 1930s progressed, that hypocrisy played an increasingly central rhetorical role in Plaid Cymru's argument against those that it suspected of preparing the way for another world war. The following passage, from Saunders Lewis's contribution to the November 1938 edition of *Y Ddraig Goch*, illustrates the kind of logic that was deployed:

> A number of Welsh religious conferences over the past few months have passed motions protesting against the cruel incarceration in Germany of [the famous Protestant theologian Martin] Niemöller. They are to be commended for doing so, although I cannot recall that they ever passed similar unanimous motions when the English government was throwing Gandhi into prison, or his followers in their thousands and hundreds of thousands.[18]

It should be emphasised that Lewis believed unequivocally that the manner in which Niemöller had been treated was completely unacceptable. His doubts concerned the moral right of some of those Welshmen who condemned his treatment to do so when they so conspicuously failed to consider the beam in their own eye, so to speak. Following the declaration of war, the party considered 'exposing the hypocrisy of England's war aims . . . a very important part of . . . [its] mission.[19]

These words were written in the wake of the Soviet Union's Winter War with Finland, an act of aggression in flagrant contravention of international law and yet one that the United Kingdom and its allies did nothing of any consequence to oppose. This despite the rhetoric about the importance of defending 'small nations' that had resounded around the time of the declaration of war against

Germany just a few months previously. The rights, the lands and the lives of the people of Finland were sacrificed on the altar of realpolitik. There was indeed a great deal of hypocrisy implicit in the positions and actions of the British state during the war years.[20] But in his belief that this hypocrisy should be exposed, Saunders Lewis went a step further, equating Fascism and Nazism with British imperialism. Yes, Hitler's conduct was horrific and, indeed, diabolical; but so too England's conduct during the years of exploitation and oppression in which it built the British Empire. Indeed, given his belief that one of the primary causes of the war was 'Power Politics in the service of greed' – 'Competition for markets, control of raw materials, and the maintenance of living standards or the achievement of higher living standards than in other countries' – Saunders Lewis considered that Nazi Germany was simply following in tracks already pioneered by nineteenth century British imperialism. Both sides were equally morally culpable – not for abstract reasons alone, but also because of Britain's behaviour towards its colonies.

In the weekly 'Cwrs y Byd' articles we encounter suspicion of Britain's (hypocritical) war aims, suspicion of her propaganda, and suspicion of her intentions. Suspicion also of Britain's major allies: of the Soviet Union (for obvious reasons), the United States (for its base materialism (12 September 1945)) and de Gaulle ('De Gaulle's economic ideas are definitively National Socialist; de Gaulle wants a strong, industrial France, with its industries at the service of French military might and the central state' (31 May 1944)).

There was, of course, much more than this to 'Cwrs y Byd' – the single most remarkable contribution ever made to Welsh journalism and political commentary. Saunders Lewis made penetrating and perceptive suggestions about the likely longer-term implications of a wide range of wartime events. For instance, he showed great insight in analysing the implications of Japan's military victories for the fate of the European empires in the Far East (25 February 1942; 30 December 1942). It is likely that many, by now, would agree with his criticism of the conduct of the Allied bombing of Germany in the closing months of the war (27 December 1944). Rereading the column also serves as a reminder that its author was as fallible as the rest of us when it came to predictions. This should hardly be a surprise given that he was attempting to follow world events from his home in Llanfarian near Aberystwyth, making the best use that he could of whatever news sources that were available. Nevertheless, some of his misreadings reveal much about his prejudices. So, for example, consistent with his belief that there was a fundamental affinity between Nazism and Communism, he refused to entertain the possibility that Hitler might ever invade the Soviet Union (19 October 1939; 23 April 1941).

In terms of broader political significance, however – and of long-term impact on the reputation of its author and his party – it is the suspicion with which England/Britain were viewed, combined with the tendency to equate British imperialism with Fascism, that were the most significant characteristics of 'Cwrs y Byd' (as well as Plaid Cymru's own literature) during the Second World War. For the party's opponents, they were proof that Plaid Cymru could never be trusted and, indeed, that it should be cast into the political wilderness via the grotesque accusation of Fascism (as attempted by Thomas Jones, Gwilym Davies et al). Even in the eyes of some of the party's supporters, its position seemed ill-judged: could the condemnation of imperialism in all its forms not be accompanied by a recognition that German imperialism was a greater threat to Wales than the British equivalent, thus allowing support for the war efforts of England and France? This was the question posed by a local Welsh Nationalist Party official to the party's General Secretary, J. E. Jones.[21] The questioner might have added that the author of 'Cwrs y Byd' would not have survived long in Germany or Italy if he had attempted to publish views that were so consistently critical of their governing regimes.

Some within Plaid Cymru sought to placate whatever misgivings they may have had about their party's stance by arguing that its position vis-à-vis the war was the same as Gandhi's or that of the Irish government.[22] The comparison was far from sound, however. Gandhi took advantage of the crisis in which the British Empire was mired in order to launch his famous 'quit India' campaign. De Valera, even though he resisted Ireland's entry into the war, ensured that the Free State leaned towards the Allies – at least, once it became clear which way the international wind was blowing. More fundamentally, the political situation faced by the Welsh nationalists of Plaid Cymru on the one hand, and nationalists in India and Ireland on the other, bore no comparison. Rather than being a powerful mass movement numbering millions, or the government of a sovereign state, Welsh nationalists were a tiny fringe group; a group whose voice would inevitably be drowned out if it attempted to stand against the violent tides swirling around it. It is no surprise that the refusal to stand alongside Britain (and the Dominions among whose number the party hoped that Wales might one day be counted) was interpreted as support for Britain's enemies. This was not the case: Plaid Cymru's self-proclaimed neutrality was exactly that. A degree of pragmatism would, though, have been much the wiser course. Indeed, were Gandhi and 'Dev' themselves not pragmatic in their response to war, even if that meant pursuing very different courses of action in the context of their particular circumstances?

It is, nonetheless, almost certainly futile to imagine that Plaid Cymru could ever have adopted an alternative position. So many factors conspired together to ensure that its standpoint towards the war was over determined. As has already been noted, the belief that war itself was the main enemy was held right across the party: from the numerous pacifist contingent to former soldiers such as Saunders Lewis, a man who had experienced war at its most bloody and brutal in the trenches of the Great War. Additionally, the party founders' deep suspicion of the British Empire had further intensified in the bitterness that followed Penyberth. But, above all else, Plaid Cymru was a party deliberately founded to wean Welsh nationalism from its former obsession with pragmatism and compromise. Whereas Liberals, and subsequently Labourites, had been prepared time and again to set aside their nationalist convictions for the sake of 'practicality' and 'unity', H. R. Jones, Evan Alwyn Owen, Saunders Lewis, D. J. Williams, Lewis Valentine and their like were determined that the new party would be unyielding in its testimony on behalf of those things that they regarded as vital if Wales was to secure a national future. For this first generation of leaders, fundamental principle was to be privileged above the convenient and 'reasonable' whatever the cost. The political cost of Plaid Cymru's stand during the decade of warfare spanning the mid-1930s and the mid-1940s was, however, very high indeed.

5

Welsh Political Culture

'No party can throw a stone at another. No party comes clean.'[1] These are the words of the great Labour leader, Ernest Bevin, reflecting on the attitudes of the British political parties towards international affairs during the interwar years. His was a fair and accurate verdict. What is interesting in the present context is the fact that the sins of Plaid Cymru (actual or alleged) during the 1930s have received and continue to receive a disproportionate amount of attention in comparison to the behaviour of other political parties. Who, after all, reproaches contemporary Liberal Democrats for the policies and positions of a party icon such as Lloyd George? Is Labour criticised for its naivety regarding Nazi Germany, or for its votes against rearmament, or for its actual stance on the Spanish Civil War, or, indeed, for the sympathy that existed among some of its supporters for the Soviet Union? And so on. There are multiple examples of behaviour from the period which one might use to castigate the main parties should one wish to do so. The point to note is that Plaid Cymru seems consistently to have been judged according to very different criteria from these political opponents. Plaid Cymru has been condemned in a manner that is either entirely unfair – on the basis of accusations that are utterly unfounded – or for errors that were common across the political spectrum.[2] Put simply, double standards are being applied. How might this be explained?

How, indeed, do we account for the fact that the alleged 'Fascism' of Plaid Cymru has received far more attention than the interwar electoral success of actual Fascists in Wales? At the 1931 general election, the New Party candidate Sellick Davies won over 10,000 votes in Merthyr Tydfil. The New Party had been founded by Oswald Mosley after he had left the Labour Party, and it was on a clearly Fascist trajectory by 1931.[3] The party enjoyed its biggest success in Merthyr. It succeeded in harvesting more votes in that single constituency than the total number of votes cast for Plaid Cymru in every parliamentary election it contested before 1945. Jeffrey Hamm from Ebbw Vale was an active member of the British Union of Fascists (BUF), and became one of Mosley's most trusted lieutenants in the years following the Second World War.[4] It seems probable that Glyn Williams was also a Welshman. It was Williams who introduced military uniforms, salutes, flags and badges to the New Party youth movement that would go on to form the core of the BUF's Blackshirts. One might expect that any serious reckoning with Fascism in Wales would give due attention to that remarkable result in Merthyr or to the likes of Davies, Hamm and Williams. The fact is, however, that almost nothing has been written about them.[5] Indeed, it is hard not to conclude that there has been an almost wilful reluctance to engage with the historical facts about Fascism in Wales.[6] Instead it seems that commentators have found it easier and somehow more reassuring to focus their attention on a party that, whatever its failings, was constant in its *opposition* to Fascism.

There are doubtless several explanations for this. For one thing, the longevity of the accusations is testimony to Plaid Cymru's ineffectiveness in responding to critics. It is as though the party has never understood that the endless repetition of such wild accusations, based on such shaky factual foundations, could actually leave a permanent mark. In this regard, Plaid Cymru has been politically naïve. Which raises, in turn, a point of more general significance: to research the history of Plaid Cymru is to be struck by the extent to which, through the years, there has been something rather naïve and even apolitical about the way in which the majority of the party's membership has approached the political realm. For those unaware of the party's history and its particular internal culture, this might appear a rather strange assertion. Who, after all, has ever heard of an unpolitical or apolitical political party? Nonetheless, as has been noted elsewhere, Plaid Cymru members long regarded Welsh nationalism as more a crusade than a conventional political cause.[7] This was a party that defiantly took its distance from the mainstream of British politics in Wales, rejecting some of its most basic assumptions. As a result, the rules of the conventional political game have sometimes appeared alien to it; the kinds of realpolitik concerns that (inevitably) preoccupy the mainstream have been deemed somehow irrelevant.[8] There is no doubt that this aspect of the party's character and culture is something that most Plaid Cymru members have regarded as a real virtue, even if it has done nothing to aid in the task of building mass support.

Another far more sinister explanation for the tenacity of the accusation of Fascism against Plaid Cymru is that it is further testimony to the truth of that chilling and desperately cynical claim by Hitler's arch-propagandist, Joseph Goebbels, namely that the frequent repetition of a big lie will generate its own truth. After more than sixty years of repetition, the alleged 'extremism' of Plaid Cymru before and during the Second World War is now regarded by many in Wales as a self-evident truth. Indeed, my own anecdotal experience would suggest that a great many, if not the majority, of current Plaid Cymru members actually believe it.

In my view, however, the real significance of the accusation of Fascism made against Plaid Cymru lies in the way that it both reflects and manifests crucial aspects of Welsh political culture. Indeed, the accusation would make a revealing case study for a broader investigation of the pathologies of that political culture. Such an investigation lies beyond the scope of the present volume, but an attempt will nonetheless be made in what follows to draw attention to some relevant considerations.

Focusing first on some of the more historical aspects, it is clear from the foregoing that the accusation of Fascism made against Plaid Cymru has been suffused with the anti-Catholicism that was once such a prominent feature of Welsh culture – political culture as well as popular culture. Indeed, the accusation may well be the last distant echo of that ancient prejudice to have lingered into the present day. Even if those politicians and journalists who continue to accuse Plaid Cymru of Fascist tendencies or of having a Fascist past are not themselves anti-Catholic, much of what they have to say about the alleged 'Fascism' of Plaid Cymru stems directly – unbeknownst to them, to be sure – from the crude anti-Catholic prejudices of an earlier generation of accusers such as Gwilym Davies and W. J. Gruffydd. They would do well to ponder this, particularly given that – and this is the great irony – Catholics have been prominent on the most unreconstructedly unionist wing of the Labour Party in Wales; that is the section of the party that has been most ready to direct accusations of Fascism at Welsh nationalists.

If anti-Catholic sentiment has largely dissipated in the years since the Second World War, the latter conflict provided a means of rearticulating and strengthening British nationalism. This is another relevant aspect of Welsh political culture to be considered as we seek to understand the longevity of the unfounded accusations of Fascism against Plaid Cymru.

There can be no doubt that Britishness experienced a renaissance after 1939. Following a period in which it stood 'alone' against Hitler's hordes – to adopt a suitably Churchillian tone – the British Empire played a largely honourable part alongside the Soviet Union and the United States in the great struggle to defeat and rid the world of Nazism. Then, as the war drew to its close, the remarkable result of the 1945 general election saw Churchill and his party swept aside by an electorate desirous of more than simply an end to the conflict. A Labour government was elected with a mandate to transform the timid state of the 1930s – a state that had effectively 'passed by on the other side' as society was being ravaged by the impact of the Great Depression – into a state that took active responsibility for its citizenry; into a *welfare* state. New institutions and organisations were established, most notably the Health Service, that would go on to enjoy cross-party support. The term 'Butskellism' was coined to describe the post-war political consensus ushered in by Labour's reform. This term combined the names of two successive Chancellors, Labour's Hugh Gaitskell and the Conservatives' Rab Butler, standing as a sign of the way that the ideological chasm between Right and Left had ostensibly been bridged. What underpinned and, indeed, made possible this ideological fusion, was a new national pride and unity. Britain had not only been successful in war, but it appeared also to have succeeded in peacetime in creating what the architects of the Swedish welfare state called a *folkhem* – a home for all the people. After all, it was not only a Health Service that was created; it was a *National* Health Service. Little wonder that Britishness was riding high in the 1950s. Little wonder either that, given the desperate privations of the 1930s, British nationalism attained a particular apotheosis in post-war Wales.

With British nationalism enjoying common-sense, taken-for-granted status – and with the fundamental normative 'goodness' of Britishness also apparently beyond doubt – there was little truck with and even less welcome for the alternative nationalism of Plaid Cymru. Particularly so as the party had opposed precisely that which had given Britain its self-respect and its (perhaps under-standable) sense of moral authority: namely the role it had played in the Second World War. From this perspective, attitudes in the interwar period did not matter. The illusions and delusions, omissions and commissions of the period before 3 September 1939 could all be forgiven and forgotten. What mattered were attitudes after the moment that Britain declared war on Germany. As we have seen, at the height of the war deliberate efforts were made by the most influential sections of the Welsh establishment to undermine and render 'beyond the pale' the beliefs of Welsh nationalists, by claiming those beliefs were synonymous with Fascism. Considering the status of British nationalism in the years following the war, it should not surprise us that the attacks on Plaid Cymru continued. If the continuing condemnation of Welsh nationalism is testimony to the hegemonic hold of British nationalist assumptions on Welsh political culture, the particular form of those attacks – namely the accusation of Fascism – speaks to the signal importance of the fight against Nazi Germany to the self-image and self-understanding of British nationalism after 1939.

One further aspect of Welsh political culture is relevant when considering claims regarding the alleged Fascist past of Plaid Cymru. Since the dawning of the democratic era in the second half of the nineteenth century, one-party dominance has provided *the* defining feature of Welsh electoral politics. The Liberal hegemony that prevailed prior to 1914 was replaced after an interwar interregnum by similarly dominant Labour performances. One-party domination is an unusual phenomenon in democratic societies, and yet it has received no more than passing mention to date: a reflection, no doubt, of the scant scholarly attention that has been paid to Welsh politics in general.[9] A number of factors explain the genesis and persistence of one-party domination in Wales, among them the country's economic structure and the way in which national and class narratives have intertwined to create the myth of a one-class nation. In addition, it must also be recalled that electoral politics in Wales is distorted by a voting system that has led on occasion to some of the least proportional results ever seen in a modern democracy![10] Needless to say, it is the largest party that benefits most from this lack of proportionality.

But setting aside the causes of one-party domination, what have been its consequences?[11] In the absence (until comparatively recently) of democratic Welsh political institutions other than at the level of local government, it could be argued that the country has been spared some of the worst effects associated with one-party domination. Without them, the kind of institutionalised corruption that we associate with Northern Ireland between 1921 and 1972, for example, or with Japan under the influence of the Liberal Democratic Party, was impossible. But if Wales has been spared some of the more typical side effects of one-party domination thanks to the absence of democratic institutions, other baleful consequences may have become exaggerated. Among them is the tendency to reduce all politics to electoral competition, particularly where the workings of the first-past-the-post system used in Westminster elections mean that it's a case of winner takes all. Here political opponents are not regarded as indispensable parts of a wider political context, but are rather viewed as enemies to be smashed and obliterated – figuratively if not literally. In one of his most famous statements, Aneurin Bevan spoke of his 'deep burning hatred for the Tory Party'. This seems to me to be a particularly Welsh political affectation. There were certainly Tories in London in whose company and hospitality Bevan revelled. But back in Wales, without the institutions within which political opponents were forced to work alongside each other and where elections counted for all, there was no reason to develop a system of values that privileged political pluralism. And in such a context, the accusation of Fascism became the convenient club with which to pulverize a potential threat. After all, what better way to silence or marginalise alternative voices than to link them with Hitler and his works? Furthermore, the absence of political institutions ensured that the other underpinnings necessary to encourage the kind of broad debate essential for any mature democracy could not develop in Wales, such as a plurality of press and media sources, relevant academic research and teaching. Given these factors, who was in a position to scrutinise and challenge the claims of the largest party?

All that being said, when we consider the longevity, not to mention the vitriol, of the accusations of Fascism laid against Plaid Cymru, there would still seem to be a 'surplus' here that is beyond rational explanation. Bearing in mind quite how marginal an electoral force Plaid Cymru was in the years before devolution, the anger that it has managed to provoke among its opponents appears excessive and unreasonable; at times, in fact, it has bordered on the hysterical. In such circumstances, the conceptual armoury of conventional political science appears inadequate to the task of explaining and understanding. Perhaps the key lies in the field of psychology? Lacking expertise in that particular discipline, I will rather offer two observations that should be regarded as no more than suggestions or hypotheses.

The first concerns the position of Saunders Lewis in the cultural life of modern Wales.

Lewis was, without doubt, the greatest scandal of twentieth-century Wales. It was not only that century which he discomforted. We have seen how tarring the name of Saunders Lewis was central to the campaign waged by the *Welsh Mirror* against Welsh nationalists at the start of the twenty-first.[12] Whatever nonsense is spouted about him in the present day, Lewis's great sin – his original sin, so to speak – was to challenge the dominant, monolithic view in Wales about what it meant to be 'truly' Welsh. This was a view that had become calcified by the late nineteenth century and which depicted Wales as being democratic in its sociology and 'radical' in its politics. This was the idea of Welshness embodied in the myth of the *Gwerin* and in its successor myth of the Welsh Working Class; this idea of Welshness was common ground between the Liberal philosopher Sir Henry Jones and the Communist novelist Lewis Jones.[13]

By stark contrast, in an undoubtedly unintentional echo of the Austro-Marxist, Otto Bauer, Saunders Lewis insisted that a nation without its own bourgeoisie was doomed to assimilation.[14] Lewis insisted that Conservatism and Welshness were compatible. He even insisted that forms of Christian belief other than Protestant Nonconformity were compatible with Welshness. To crown it all, he insisted that the Welsh language could and should be the language of politics and civil administration, as well as the language of hearth and chapel. In the context of the dominant understandings of Welshness that prevailed at that time, it is impossible to imagine a more iconoclastic position than Saunders Lewis's conservative, Catholic, Welsh-language-centred aristocratism (*uchelwriaeth*). Yet, because of Lewis's intellectual stature and moral authority, he could not simply be ignored. Instead, an attempt was made to discredit his ideas totally by linking them with Fascism; an accusation that not only betrays profound ignorance of Lewis's thinking, but an equally profound ignorance of the broader intellectual context of the interwar years.

Among the most memorable one-liners in the entire *oeuvre* of Tom Nairn – a body of work rich in the wise, pithy and provocative – is his observation in 1968 that Scotland would never be free 'until the last minister [of the Presbyterian kirk] has been strangled with the last copy of the *Sunday Post*'. His point, of course, was that the church and the popular press were conservative forces – one might even say reactionary forces – that served to shrink and limit the horizons of his fellow countrymen. If we transpose this comment into the Welsh context and, in a manner of speaking, turn it on its head, it would seem to me that the way in which we treat the ideas and legacy of our most important home-grown Conservative provides us with an important yardstick. Not to measure the degree of our national 'freedom', perhaps, but rather to measure the state of our nation's intellectual health. Wales will have an intellectual life worthy of the name when it finally becomes possible to discuss the ideas of Saunders Lewis in all their complexity without the accusation of Fascism casting its dark and debilitating shadow.

The second point takes us back to an issue discussed at length in the opening chapter of the first volume of my lengthier study of the ideas of Plaid Cymru, *Rhoi Cymru'n Gyntaf: Syniadaeth Plaid Cymru* (2007). An argument that is, in fact, central to the understanding of nationalism that underpins the study in its entirety. I refer to the absolutely central role of nationalism in the politics of the contemporary world.

For good and ill, no doubt, the sovereign nation-state is the basic unit of international politics. Understanding how the two elements of the compound noun 'nation-state' relate to each other is key if we are to understand why this form of political and administrative organisation has proven so attractive – certainly when compared with alternative methods of organisation such as empire, for example. Rooted in the early modern era, the idea that the validity, credibility and legitimacy of a particular polity depends on its ability to operate as the expression of the will of a nation has achieved 'common sense' status. This is in part, at least, because the willingness of citizens to contribute voluntarily of their blood and treasure to this national form of political organisation has allowed it prove more resilient than every alternative. The equation (indeed, conflation) of nation and state has come to be regarded as entirely natural. Unless a state is founded on a nation, it is unlikely to survive – unless it can create a sense of nationhood to underpin itself. And if a nation lacks its own state . . .? This brings us to the interestingly ambivalent case of Wales.

Space precludes full and detailed examination of the evidence here, but when we consider the situation as it has prevailed since the end of the nineteenth century onwards, there can be little doubt that the vast majority of the people of Wales have regarded Britain as a nation and Great Britain as a nation-state. Doubtless they have also been patriotic Britons themselves. But at the same time, we can be confident that a majority have also thought of Wales as a nation and of themselves as patriotic Welshmen and women.[15] There is thus no simple way of rendering the Welsh experience consistent with the modern-day norm of one nation, one state. Obviously this is something that has not troubled most of the people most of the time. There have been other priorities and lives to live. When forced to consider the matter, however, is it not inevitable that a large measure of unease has been in evidence? How indeed given the fundamental assumptions regarding political organisation in the modern world, is it possible to reconcile a sense of Welsh nationhood, on the one hand, with opposition to the idea of self-government for Wales, on the other? And is it not the apparent contradiction at the heart of this position, and the discomfort that it has created, that has given rise to outraged statements to the effect that 'I'm as Welsh as you are' – and dozens of variations on that theme – routinely thrown in the face of Welsh nationalists by their opponents? This perhaps goes some way to explaining the vitriolic attacks provoked by Welsh nationalism even when 'y Blaid bach' – 'the small party', as it was condescendingly known to many Welsh speakers – was genuinely tiny. In a world of nationalism and nation-states, and in the context of Wales's ambivalent condition, Welsh nationalists, however few their numbers, were promoting an agenda that could only generate a sense of unease, bitterness and even anger among their fellow countrymen. This is the anger that has prompted some to go so far as to try to link Welsh nationalists with one of the darkest, most depraved episodes in human history in order that they might be silenced.

6

Conclusion: Redemption and Exclusion

One year after the first National Assembly election, with the *Welsh Mirror* cranking up its campaign against Welsh nationalists, Jan Morris published a short novel titled *Our First Leader: A Welsh Fable*. A few months later a superbly rendered Welsh-language version appeared, prepared by Morris's son, Twm Morys, titled *Ein Llyw Cyntaf*.[1] The novel satirises the notion that Wesh nationalists were Fascist sympathisers and fellow travellers. Morris's counter factual history imagines a Second World War from which the United States and Japan had remained aloof, and in which Britain has been forced to surrender and has been occupied by Nazi forces. Following the occupation, the Germans establish a Welsh colony – *Cymru Newydd* (New Wales) – in Meirionnydd and Montgomeryshire. This colony is partly populated by repatriating to Wales sections of the Welsh diaspora that had fled to the towns and cities of England during the interwar years in order to escape the effects of the Depression. A Welsh nationalist and academic named Dr Parry-Morris is invited to be the leader – '*Y Llyw*' – of *Cymru Newydd*. It is unclear whether the author's description of Parry-Morris is deliberately meant to evoke any particular individual, but bearing in mind who was seen (by his opponents) as the person most likely to be willing to govern Wales 'according to the totalitarian principle' (as W. J. Gruffydd put it), it is hard to resist the temptation of identifying him with the figure of Saunders Lewis.

It rapidly becomes apparent that the Nazis' plans for the population of their protectorate are terrifyingly sinister. Having first wrung as much labour as possible from their malnourished bodies in factories producing weapons to satisfy the apparently insatiable demand of the Russian front (where the Soviet Union and Germany remain locked in a merciless, intractable war), the racially suspect Welsh are to be sent to an 'Honour Home' in Snowdonia: in reality, gas chambers in Llanberis. Meanwhile, at least for a time, *Cymru Newydd* has one other function to fulfil. The colony is to be used as a kind of Potemkin village in a cynical public relations effort designed to convince US television cameras that life in Britain is tolerable enough even under the Reich. Such is Parry-Morris's desire to exploit the German victory for his own nationalist ends that he and his followers seem prepared to submit willingly to Nazi demands – as, of course, so many other nationalists the length and breadth of Europe had done in the early 1940s. Parry-Morris appears more concerned with protocol and the trappings of power in his new puppet state than with looming national extinction; harping on to all and sundry about the genius of medieval Welsh literature rather than worrying about the present and the future of his own nation, let alone the rest of humanity.

Parry-Morris's formal title, *Y Llyw* (for which leader is the best English approximation), is extremely suggestive. It invokes Llywelyn ap Gruffudd (*c.*1225–82), known to Welsh speakers as *Llywelyn ein Llyw Olaf*, the last native Prince prior to the final conquest of Wales. As well as invoking Llywelyn ap Gruffudd, it is however a title with much more contemporary resonance. The title assumed by Hitler, *der Führer*, translates as *Y Llyw* and so, even more appositely, does the title adopted by the Norwegian whose name became a byword for treason, Vidkun Quisling, who was known to his followers as the *Fører*.

There is, though, a twist in the tail of the novel. The *Llyw* is no Welsh Quisling, after all. Rather we discover that Parry-Morris is in fact a shrewd strategist who uses his fame and status, developed as a result of his apparently faithful service to the Nazis' New Order, to draw the Americans into the war. Through his conspiring, *Cymru Newydd* becomes a stepping-stone for an all-out American military assault that succeeds in liberating Europe. Far from being a traitor, Parry-Morris is a leader who not only rescues and redeems his own people, but facilitates the rescue and redemption of a continent.

Set alongside the sophistry, prejudice and barefaced lies that have characterised the accusation of Fascist sympathies laid against Plaid Cymru, Jan Morris's deftly constructed and (despite the subject matter) witty tale comes as a breath of fresh air. Nevertheless, however acclaimed the author, one satirical novel is hardly likely to shake the now deeply-rooted belief that Plaid Cymru is somehow tainted by association with Fascism. There is simply no substance to this claim. If we believe that the term 'Fascist' is more than some casual, indiscriminate term of abuse to be directed against those that happen to transgress us, but is rather a meaningful reference to a body of ideas that came to prominence in the twentieth century, and which is associated above all with Mussolini's Italy and Hitler's Germany, then the accusation of Fascism directed at Plaid Cymru must be totally rejected. There was and is nothing Fascist about the ideas and standpoints of the party and its leadership. The appropriate way to understand and interpret this accusation is not as a commentary on or analysis of Welsh nationalism, but rather as a deliberate attempt to exclude Plaid Cymru from the sphere of acceptable political discourse in Wales – to render the party and its ideas 'beyond the pale'. It is an exclusionary strategy that has, of course, enjoyed a substantial measure of success. Thus while few things are certain in the world of politics, based on the experience of the past eighty or so years, we can predict with confidence that whenever public opinion swings again towards Plaid Cymru, the same old accusation will resurface. After all, it has, to date, proven a highly effective means of thwarting the party's rise.

That said even if the accusation is one day revived and relaunched, is there perhaps room to hope – to dare to hope – that its reception might this time be different? Wales and its political culture have certainly changed substantially, even compared to the period only a decade or so ago when the *Welsh Mirror* spewed its poison about Welsh nationalism. At that time, the Labour Party in Wales remained deeply divided on the issue of devolution, with a strong faction in its ranks still sceptical of any steps in the direction of self-government. This faction centred, of course, on the Welsh Parliamentary Labour Party at Westminster; a group thoroughly inculcated in the habits, expectations and prejudices of one-partyism. By now, however, things have changed with the so-called devo-sceptics no longer the force they once were. This change is to a very large extent due to the way in which the balance of power among the elected representatives of Wales's largest party has shifted from the banks of the Thames to the shores of Cardiff Bay. This process was crystallised above all, perhaps, in the decision of the Wales Labour Party to form a coalition with Plaid Cymru after the 2007 Assembly election, leading to the formation of the 'One Wales' government. This was a development bitterly opposed by the majority of Labour MPs in Wales, along with key members of the party's *ancien régime* such as Neil Kinnock, but supported by the Labour Group in the National Assembly and the overwhelming majority of rank and file members in the constituencies.

The semi-proportional electoral system used for the National Assembly would have been enough in itself to prompt a change in attitudes. For the first time, coalition building has become a central and, indeed, indispensable aspect of Welsh politics. It is unlikely that a stable government will ever be possible at the devolved level without some measure of understanding (informal or formal) between two or more of the political parties involved. In a situation such as this, keeping options open is a prerequisite for political effectiveness. From the Labour Party's point of view – and it is Labour, of course, that has been the source of the most vitriolic accusations of Fascism against Plaid Cymru – alienating Welsh nationalists by seeking to identify them with Hitler and Mussolini has become self-defeating. Over the longer term, such allegations will only serve to poison relationships and thus weaken Labour's own bargaining position in Cardiff.

It is not only institutions and voting systems that have changed. By now many of the most basic elements of the Welsh nationalist credo – ideas that were once considered eccentric, reactionary or even Fascist – have become part of the political mainstream in Wales. Who in the contemporary Welsh political life would be prepared to state publicly that they did not believe Wales to be a nation and, therefore, that it should not be considered as a 'natural' administrative and political unit? Who would be prepared to state publicly that Wales should not be granted at least some degree of self-government? Who, indeed, would be willing to argue that Wales should not at least aspire to being a bilingual nation? Even if the accusations of Fascism have been successful in thwarting Plaid Cymru, they have not succeeded in preventing the process via which the most fundamental tenets of Welsh nationalism have come to enjoy hegemonic status. Within such a context, it is likely that any renewed attempt to equate Welsh nationalism with Fascism would cause discomfort for more than simply supporters of Plaid Cymru. This because the reputation of all those small 'n' Welsh nationalists who are now to be found in every unionist party would also be at stake. It is worth reminding ourselves that there were many outside Plaid Cymru who were pleased at the demise of the *Welsh Mirror*. Although party allegiance meant that devolutionists within Labour were spared some of the opprobrium heaped upon Plaid Cymru leaders and supporters, they nonetheless also found themselves on the receiving end of the tabloid's scorn.

Only time will tell when and in what context someone will attempt to resuscitate the accusation that Plaid Cymru is tainted by association with Fascism. Whatever our specific views of the party's policies and aims, anyone with the slightest interest in seeing Wales develop a vigorous and effective democracy must surely hope that the Welsh electorate will refuse to offer them a hearing. The greatest imperative in Welsh politics is to nurture a pluralistic political culture in which different views and voices are heard and engaged with in a serious and mature way. Within such a culture, the ideas of Plaid Cymru – and every other democratic political party – would quite rightly be subject to criticism and challenge. Much of the electorate, perhaps the majority, would likely reject them. They would do so, however, not on the basis of some grotesque and fundamentally untruthful accusation that those ideas are somehow tainted by Fascism, but rather because they fail to convince in their own right. Such is the nature of politics in properly mature, democratic countries. One day, Wales too will join their ranks.

Notes

1 The Accusations

1 'UCW Notes', *Cambrian News*, 25 November 1938, p. 7.

2 To reinforce this point, a reader of the Welsh-language version of this book contacted me to point out that Islwyn Pritchard became a member of Plaid Cymru later in life.

3 The exact relationship between Fascism and Nazism continues to be the subject of intense academic debate. It is generally accepted, however, that the latter is a specific manifestation of the former; a manifestation that as well as sharing certain characteristics with the former is distinguished by its own particular characteristics and pathologies. This issue is discussed further in chapter 3, 'Defining Fascism'.

4 *Daily Herald*, 15 February 1938. See also *Baner ac Amserau Cymru*, 22 February 1938.

5 For an excellent discussion of internal tensions within Plaid Cymru around this issue see D. Hywel Davies, *The Welsh Nationalist Party 1925–45: A Call to Nationhood* (Cardiff: University of Wales Press, 1983), pp. 112–14.

6 See Rhisiart Hinks, *E. Prosser Rhys 1901–45* (Llandysul: Gomer, 1980), pp. 126–35. For a discussion of the circumstances surrounding the founding of Plaid Cymru see Richard Wyn Jones, *Rhoi Cymru'n Gyntaf: Syniadaeth Plaid Cymru, Vol. 1* (Caerdydd: Gwasg Prifysgol Cymru, 2007), pp. 55–66.

7 Prosser Rhys, 'Led-Led Cymru', *Baner ac Amserau Cymru*, 8 March 1938, 5.

8 'It may not be an overstatement to say that on an intellectual level, *Cwrs y Byd* was the most important factor in supporting the spirit, the national morale, through the dark and pessimistic years for Welsh nationalists. Without it, the movement would have been but a shadow

of its former self by the end of the war. In *Cwrs y Byd*, the kind of neutrality of thought was fostered that would prove indispensable if the national movement was to survive.' A. O. H. Jarman, 'Y Blaid a'r Ail Ryfel Byd' (Plaid Cymru and the Second World War), John Davies (ed.), *Cymru'n Deffro: Hanes y Blaid Genedlaethol* (Talybont: Y Lolfa, 1981), p. 83.

9   D. Emrys Evans. 'Y Rhyfel a'r Dewis', *Y Llenor*, XX (2), Summer 1941, 72.

10 Evans, 'Y Rhyfel a'r Dewis', 72.

11 Evans, 'Y Rhyfel a'r Dewis', 74.

12 Evans, 'Y Rhyfel a'r Dewis', 76. The mention of a telescope here is an obvious reference to the column on international affairs published in Plaid Cymru's Welsh-language monthly *Y Ddraig Goch* throughout the 1930s titled 'Trwy'r Sbïenddrych' (Through the Telescope). The phrase 'the treason of men of letters' translates the original Welsh, 'brad y gwŷr llên', and would appear to be a deliberate invocation of the famous work by Julien Benda, *La trahison des clercs* (1927) (*The Treason of the Intellectuals*), which included an attack inter alia on Charles Maurras and Maurice Barrès (two figures to whom we shall shortly return.)

13 On 28 February 1942, the *Western Mail and South Wales News* reported the occasion under the headline 'Home Truths on Welsh Government'. The speech was published in its entirety under the title 'The Native Never Returns' in Thomas Jones, *The Native Never Returns* (London: W Griffiths & Co., 1946), pp. 9–27. Needless to say, the fact he chose to reprint the speech and use its title for the entire volume strongly suggests that his position had changed little in the intervening years.

14 Jones, *The Native Never Returns*, t. 23.

15 Jones, *The Native Never Returns*, t. 20. It would seem that this mention of Denmark, Grundtvig and, indeed, adult education are references to the efforts by D. J. and Noëlle Davies in the 1930s to establish a Folk High School on Scandinavian lines (an episode to which I return in the forthcoming second volume of *Syniadaeth Plaid Cymru*). But Plaid Cymru's interest in Denmark and Grundtvig were hardly new; it is rather that T.J. seems to have been slow in catching up with some of the party's ideas. As for the Urdd, T.J. had been in correspondence with its founder and leader, Ifan ab Owen Edwards, to suggest inviting the then Princess Elizabeth to be patron of the movement. Edwards agreed with the idea, noting the added advantage that such an arrangement might have in silencing 'extreme' nationalists. E. L. Ellis, *T.J.: A Life of Dr Thomas Jones* (Cardiff: University of Wales Press, 1992), p. 458.

16 See Ellis, *T.J.: A Life of Dr Thomas Jones*, pp. 380–421. See also the following assessment of T.J. by William R. Rock in his volume *British Appeasement*

in the 1930s (London: Edward Elgar, 1977), p. 64: 'he warrants identification . . . not as an exceptional advocate of appeasement, but because he is broadly representative of the highly placed "unofficial" Englishman [*sic*] who lent support to the policy for a time'.

17 Von Ribbentrop became one of Hitler's prominent henchmen, and was subsequently sentenced to death as a war criminal at Nuremberg. During the war, the son who had once appeared destined for Eton was an officer in the SS. See John Weitz, *Hitler's Diplomat: Joachim von Ribbentrop* (London: Phoenix Giant, 1992).

18 This is recounted in Ellis, *T.J.: A Life of Dr Thomas Jones*, pp. 412–21.

19 Ian Kershaw, *Making Friends with Hitler: Lord Londonderry and Britain's Road to War* (London: Allen Lane, 2004).

20 'Within months of Hitler's accession to power T.J. was energetically seeking assistance from British and American universities for Jewish scholars fleeing from persecution. And his efforts on behalf of refugees continued unabated down to and beyond the outbreak of war, in some cases at considerable personal expense.' Ellis, *T.J.: A Life of Dr Thomas Jones*, p. 405.

21 Gwilym Davies, 'Cymru Gyfan a'r Blaid Genedlaethol Gymreig', *Y Traethodydd*, 424 (July 1942), 97–111.

22 It would also appear that the UNESCO constitution is based on the plan originally proposed by Davies; he was also the first person to broadcast in the Welsh language. See the entry on Davies in E. D. Jones and Brynley F. Roberts (eds), *Y Bywgraffiadur Cymreig 1951–1970* (Llundain: Anrhydeddus Gymdeithas y Cymmrodorion, 1997), p. 29.

23 Davies, 'Cymru Gyfan a'r Blaid Genedlaethol Gymreig', 101.

24 Davies, 'Cymru Gyfan a'r Blaid Genedlaethol Gymreig', 102.

25 Davies, 'Cymru Gyfan a'r Blaid Genedlaethol Gymreig', 103.

26 Davies, 'Cymru Gyfan a'r Blaid Genedlaethol Gymreig', 99.

27 Davies, 'Cymru Gyfan a'r Blaid Genedlaethol Gymreig', 107.

28 Davies, 'Cymru Gyfan a'r Blaid Genedlaethol Gymreig', 105.

29 Davies, 'Cymru Gyfan a'r Blaid Genedlaethol Gymreig', 105.

30 Davies, 'Cymru Gyfan a'r Blaid Genedlaethol Gymreig', 106.

31 Davies, 'Cymru Gyfan a'r Blaid Genedlaethol Gymreig', 105.

32 Davies, 'Cymru Gyfan a'r Blaid Genedlaethol Gymreig', 110.

33 Davies, 'Cymru Gyfan a'r Blaid Genedlaethol Gymreig', 111.

34 Davies was not the first prominent figure in Nonconformist Wales to use the supposed Catholicism of Plaid Cymru as the main line of attack in branding the party as sympathetic to Fascism. See, for example, the exchanges between the Revd R. H. Hughes, Manchester, and J. E. Daniel in the May 1938 edition of *Y Ddraig Goch*, under the headline 'Ateb Cyhuddiad o Ffasgaeth' (Response to an Accusation of Fascism).

35 For the purposes of this chapter, I shall not discuss in detail the claim that Maurras was the father of Fascism and that *L'Action Française* was a Fascist organisation. Unless it can be demonstrated that Maurras and *Action Française* were the main influences on Plaid Cymru's political philosophy, as Gwilym Davies would have us believe, or at least that they were a significant influence, then the nature of the ideas of *Action Française* and its founder is of no relevance to the present discussion. It should be noted, however, that the relation between the ideas of *Action Française* and Fascism remains an issue of real contention among academics. There are certainly some who would tend to agree with Davies in arguing that France was the seedbed of Fascism. See, for example, Zeev Sternhell, *Neither Left nor Right: Fascist Ideology in France*, trans. David Maisel (London: University of California Press, 1986), which argues that Fascist ideas permeated French politics during the interwar years. The academic consensus, however, appears to maintain a different position, namely that *Action Française* was not a Fascist organisation, and that Maurras was certainly not the father of Fascism. For one thing, the emphasis of Maurras and *Action Française* on a return to a past order is not compatible with the typical Fascist emphasis on modernity and the recreation of man *de novo*. Maurras and *Action Française* are normally considered to form part of the reactionary radical right rather than as Fascists. Eugen Weber provides his standard account in *Action Française: Royalism and Reaction in Twentieth Century France* (Stanford: Stanford University Press, 1962). That said, there can be no doubt that the ideas embraced by Maurras and his followers were deeply objectionable. Most obviously, anti-Semitism was central to Maurras's world view.

36 The slim volume that Bebb published, recounting his experiences in France and Brittany in the days leading up to the outbreak of war, *Dydd-lyfr Pythefnos, neu y Ddawns Angau* (Diary of a Fortnight, or the Dance of Death) (Bangor: Sackville Printing Works, 1939) – perhaps the most lucid example of *reportage* ever published in the Welsh language – provides indisputable evidence of the author's opposition to the Nazis. Bebb fiercely opposes the position of one faction among Breton nationalists who believed that a Nazi occupation of France would help their cause (pp. 17–30, 61–9). It is important to note, however, that his fiercely anti-Nazi and anti-German stance runs parallel with a deep admiration for Charles Maurras (pp. 7, 94) as well as a condescending attitude towards women (p. 33), Jews (p. 114) and the English (p. 128). Ambrose Bebb was a right-wing conservative, anti-Fascist Welshman; the fact that Welsh intellectual life seems to have difficulty in recognising the possibility let alone validity of such a worldview should not prevent

us from acknowledging its existence. For a discussion of Bebb's politics, see Gareth Miles, 'W. Ambrose Bebb', in Derec Llwyd Morgan (ed.), *Adnabod Deg: Portreadau o Ddeg o Arweinwyr Cynnar y Blaid Genedlaethol* (Dinbych: Gwasg Gee, 1977), pp. 77–95. See also T. Robin Chapman, *W. Ambrose Bebb* (Caerdydd: Gwasg Prifysgol Cymru, 1997)

37 Davies, 'Cymru Gyfan a'r Blaid Genedlaethol Gymreig', 99. Naturally, there were different responses among the Plaid Cymru leadership to Davies's attacks. See especially *Plaid Cymru Gyfan: Atebion Saunders Lewis a J. E. Daniel i Mr. [sic] Gwilym Davies* (The Party for all of Wales: The responses of Saunders Lewis and J. E. Daniel to Mr [sic] Gwilym Davies) (Caernarfon: Plaid Genedlaethol Cymru, 1942), which was translated by Emyr Humphreys and published (again by Plaid Cymru) under the title *The Party for Wales*. It is significant that so much of Lewis's and Daniel's responses focus on the accusation that Plaid Cymru was a 'Papist' organisation. See also Ambrose Bebb, '"Cymru Gyfan a'r Blaid Genedlaethol Gymreig": Ateb i'r Parch. Gwilym Davies' ('All of Wales and the National Party of Wales': A response to the Revd Gwilym Davies), *Y Traethodydd*, 426 (January 1943), pp. 1–14, and Gwilym Davies, '"Cymru'n Ddwy?" Ateb i Mr Ambrose Bebb' ('Wales Divided?': A response to Mr Ambrose Bebb), *Y Traethodydd*, 427 (April 1943), pp. 74–88.

38 Davies, 'Cymru Gyfan a'r Blaid Genedlaethol Gymreig', 102.

39 Saunders Lewis, 'Undebau Llafur' (Trades Unions), *Y Ddraig Goch*, November 1932.

40 Davies, 'Cymru Gyfan a'r Blaid Genedlaethol Gymreig', 106.

41 On the nature of second chambers, see *inter alia* Samuel C. Patterson and Anthony Mughan, *Senates; Bicameralism in the Contemporary World* (Columbus: Ohio State, 1999), and the special issue of the *Journal of Legislative Studies*, 7 (1) (Spring 2001).

42 A. O. H. Jarman, 'Y Blaid a'r Ail Ryfel Byd' (Plaid Cymru and the Second World War), John Davies (ed.), *Cymru'n Deffro: Hanes y Blaid Genedlaethol* (Talybont: Y Lolfa, 1981), p. 83.

43 Ellis, *T.J.: A Life of Dr Thomas Jones*, p. 460.

44 Ellis, *T.J.: A Life of Dr Thomas Jones*, p. 460.

45 Thomas Jones Archive in the National Library of Wales (H21, 24), letter to Geoffrey Dawson, *The Times*, 21 May 1941.

46 D. Francis Roberts Archive in the National Library of Wales, letter by Gwilym Davies, 17 July 1942. From this contemporary vantage point, it is noteworthy that much of the correspondence between the various accusers and their supporters (all literate in Welsh) was in English.

47 The three are given prominence in John Davies, *Broadcasting and the BBC in Wales* (Cardiff: University of Wales Press, 1994). Interestingly,

Jones had been a headmaster to and a 'great influence' on Gwynfor Evans, while Gwilym Davies had also been something of an idol for the man who would become president of Plaid Cymru; see Rhys Evans, *Gwynfor: Rhag Pob Brad* (Talybont: Y Lolfa, 2005), pp. 24, 30.

48 Gwilym Davies Archive in the National Library of Wales, letters by Edgar Jones, 3 July 1942, 5 August 1942, 1 September 1942, [n.d.], 3 April 1943. By his own admission, Edgar Jones considered his friend-ship with T.J. as one of his 'fondest possessions'. See Thomas Jones Archive in the National Library of Wales, letter by Edgar Jones, 26 October 1944.

49 D. Francis Roberts Archive in the National Library of Wales, letter by Gwilym Davies, 12 May 1942.

50 Gwilym Davies, *Cymru Gyfan a'r Blaid Genedlaethol Gymreig* (Caernarfon: Argraffdy'r Methodistiaid Calfinaidd, 1942).

51 D. Francis Roberts Archive in the National Library of Wales, letter by Gwilym Davies, 18 April 1942.

52 Gwilym Davies Archive in the National Library of Wales, letter by D. Francis Roberts, 20 July 1942.

53 Before this parliamentary constituency was abolished at the end of the 1945–50 parliament, graduates of the University of Wales had elected an MP to represent them at Westminster – yet another example of the sort of functional representation that Gwilym Davies regarded as the very essence of Fascism! In October 1942 it was announced that the sitting Liberal MP Ernest Evans would succeed Thomas Artemus Jones as county judge on the north Wales circuit, which triggered a by-election in January 1943. The most detailed discussion of the campaign is given in Tegwyn Jones, 'Etholiad y Brifysgol 1943' (The University of Wales Election 1943), *Y Faner* 2, 9, 16, 23 September 1977.

54 See T. Robin Chapman, *W. J. Gruffydd* (Caerdydd: Gwasg Prifysgol Cymru, 1993). Underlining his central role, Gruffydd's supporters sought, and received, T.J.'s approval for his candidacy. See Ellis, *T.J.: A Life of Dr Thomas Jones*, p. 462.

55 W. J. Gruffydd, 'Mae'r gwylliaid ar y ffordd' (The barbarians are coming), *Y Llenor*, October 1940, p. 116.

56 Quoted in D. Hywel Davies, *The Welsh Nationalist Party 1925–45: A Call to Nationhood*, p. 239.

57 This brings to mind a more contemporary instance of the same logic, as applied in President Bush's famous speech to Congress following the terrorist attacks on New York and Washington on 11 September 2001: 'Either you are with us, or you are with the terrorists.'

58 Trystan Owain Hughes portrays Welsh anti-Catholicism as a twentieth-century phenomenon; see Trystan Owain Hughes, *Winds of Change: The*

Roman Catholic Church and Society in Wales, 1916–92 (Cardiff: University of Wales Press, 1999). In contrast, Paul O'Leary presents ample evidence that anti-Catholicism in twentieth century Wales was a continuation of the anti-Catholicism of the nineteenth; see Paul O'Leary, 'When Was Anti-Catholicism? The Case of Nineteenth- and the Twentieth-Century Wales', *The Journal of Ecclesiastical Studies*, 56 (2) (2005), pp. 308–25.

[59] Quoted in Tegwyn Jones, 'Etholiad y Brifysgol, 1943 – (3)', *Y Faner* 16 September 1977, 11.

[60] Quoted in Jones, 'Etholiad y Brifysgol, 1943 – (3)', 12.

[61] Quoted in Jones, 'Etholiad y Brifysgol, 1943 – (3)', 12.

[62] Gruffydd, 'Mae'r gwylliaid ar y ffordd', 122–3.

[63] Gruffydd, 'Mae'r gwylliaid ar y ffordd', 123. The evidence presented in Robin Chapman's biography suggests that Gruffydd had been suspicious of the influence of Catholics in the UK's Foreign Office since 1928. The biography also provides further evidence of Gruffydd's deep antipathy towards Catholics. Following a visit to Dublin in 1936, he wrote in a letter of how he had had 'a belly full of catholics [*sic*] with their stupidity and noise and filth and ignorance'; Chapman, *W. J. Gruffydd*, p. 156. There are obvious echoes here of the anti-Semitic rhetoric of the period.

[64] Gruffydd, 'Mae'r gwylliaid ar y ffordd', 123.

[65] Gruffydd, 'Mae'r gwylliaid ar y ffordd', 124.

[66] Gruffydd, 'Mae'r gwylliaid ar y ffordd', 125. Gruffydd's reference is apparently to Cardinal Michael von Faulhaber, one of the most vocal opponents of the Nazis within the Catholic hierarchy in Germany, but a man who has also been roundly criticised since the war by observers who feel that he should have done far more in opposing Hitler's forces.

[67] Gruffydd, 'Mae'r gwylliaid ar y ffordd', 114.

[68] Gruffydd, 'Mae'r gwylliaid ar y ffordd', 126. The reference here is to the legend of 'Cantre'r Gwaelod'; a fabled lost land off the coast of Cardigan Bay that was drowned when sluice gates protecting it from the encroachment of the sea were left open by the watchman, Seithennin.

[69] See Saunders Lewis, 'Llythyr ynghylch Catholigiaeth' (Letter concerning Catholicism), *Y Llenor*, Summer 1927, 72–7; and W. J. Gruffydd, 'Atebiad y Golygydd i Mr Saunders Lewis' (Editor's response to Mr Saunders Lewis), *Y Llenor*, Summer 1927, 78–95.

[70] W. J. Gruffydd, 'Nodiadau Golygyddol' (Editorial Notes), *Y Llenor*, Winter 1940, 166.

[71] W. J. Gruffydd, 'Nodiadau Golygyddol', 168.

[72] Davies, *The Welsh Nationalist Party 1925–45: A Call to Nationhood*; A. O. H. Jarman, 'Y Blaid a'r Ail Ryfel Byd'.

[73] J. Graham Jones, 'The Parliament for Wales Campaign 1950–1956', *Welsh History Review*, 16 (2) (1992), 208. The lamp came into Edwards's possession on a visit to Buchenwald concentration camp shortly after the site was captured by Allied forces in 1945. Edwards was part of a parliamentary deputation sent to Buchenwald to ensure there were eyewitnesses to the depravities that had occured there. According to Edwards's biographer, the MP Wayne David, the lamp is now in the possession of St Martin's Comprehensive School in Caerphilly; Wayne David, *Remaining True: A Biography of Ness Edwards* (Foreword by Neil Kinnock) (Caerphilly: Caerphilly Local History Society, 2006), pp. 46–7. It is interesting to note that David does not mention Edwards' accusations of Fascism against Plaid Cymru. Rather, he frames his hero's dispute with Plaid Cymru as well as the devolutionists within his own party as a dispute between 'democracy' and 'accountability' on the one hand, and nationalism on the other (see pp. 75–89). Despite the wholly inappropriate nature of of Edwards's attacks on Welsh nationalists, we should not forget the horror of what he experienced at Buchenwald, or the enormous and lasting impact that it had on him. David's biography contains some truly appalling images of what Edwards witnessed at the camp.

[74] See Gwynfor Evans, *Bywyd Cymro*, ed. Manon Rhys (Caernarfon: Gwasg Gwynedd, 1982), p. 255.

[75] See *The Guardian*, 17 July 1968; *The Sun*, 17 July 1968. For further interesting evidence, see the letter by P. W. Enticott in *The Tribune*, 2 August 1968, 8–9.

[76] *Western Mail*, 6 January 1950, 3; see also *Baner ac Amserau Cymru*, 11 January 1950, 1.

[77] One interesting aspect of this episode is that fact that Gwilym Prys Davies – subsequently Lord Gwilym Prys Davies and unsuccessful Labour candidate in the 1966 Carmarthen by-election – was a prominent member of the Republicans. He later worked closely with Griffiths in promoting the cause of devolution within the ranks of Welsh Labour; see, for example, Richard Wyn Jones and Roger Scully, *Wales says Yes: Devolution and the 2011 Welsh Referendum* (Cardiff: University of Wales Press, 2012), pp. 28–9.

[78] The response by Plaid Cymru is given in the editorial column of *Y Ddraig Goch*, February 1950, 3.

[79] Gwynfor Evans makes several references in his various publications to the tendency among Plaid Cymru's opponents to accuse the party of Fascism or Nazism. He notes, for example, how 'this was done constantly by two Liberal candidates who stood against me in Carmarthen. The late James Griffiths called the Plaid Cymru youth section the "Hitler

Youth"; and when I first went to parliament in 1966, I was publicly welcomed as a fascist by Merlyn Rees and Ivor Richard'; Gwynfor Evans, *Diwedd Prydeindod* (Talybont: Y Lolfa, 1981), p. 45. Rees would later be promoted to Secretary of State for Northern Ireland, and then Home Secretary. In a glittering career, Richard was not only an MP but the United Kingdom's Permanent Representative on the United Nations Security Council, a European Commissioner, and Leader of the House of Lords. He would subsequently make a notable contribution to the land of his birth as chair of the Richard Commission; see Commission on the Powers and Electoral Arrangements of the National Assembly for Wales, *Report of the Richard Commission* (Cardiff: National Assembly for Wales, 2004).

80 Speech to a meeting of the 'Labour Party No Assembly' campaign at Highbury Club, Abertillery, 2 February 1979. D/g/35, Leo Abse Papers, National Library of Wales.

81 Interview with Kim Howells, 11 September 1995, BBC Scotland.

82 Interview with Kim Howells MP, 15 May 1998; Lee Waters, *From Little Acorns . . .: The Fall and Rise of Devolution in the Welsh Labour Party, 1979–1995* (Cardiff: Wales Governance Centre, 2013), p. 8.

83 *Welsh Mirror*, 22 July 2000. The headline appears above a story purportedly celebrating the publication of a pamphlet by the Labour MP Llew Smith, titled *The Language: The Cost to Wales*. There is no evidence, however, that this 'work' ever saw the light of day.

84 Patrick McGuinness provides penetrating analysis and criticism of these attacks in a series of articles published in *Planet: The Welsh Internationalist*. See 'Reflections in the "Welsh" Mirror', 153 (June/July 2002), 6–12; 'The War on Welsh: An Update', 155 (October/November 2002), 58–9; '"Racism" in Welsh Politics', 159 (June/July 2003), 7–12. See also the important essay by Simon Brooks, 'The Idiom of Race: The "Racist Nationalist" in Wales as Bogeyman', in T. Robin Chapman (ed.), *The Idiom of Dissent: Protest and Propaganda in Wales*, Foreword by Dafydd Elis-Thomas (Llandysul: Gomer, 2006), pp. 139–65.

85 Westminster Hall debate, 7 May 2002. See Column 62 WH, *Hansard*.

86 *Welsh Mirror,*16 June 2001. See also the issues of 23 February 2001, 13 April 2001, 22 May 2001, 15 June 2001, 13 July 2001, *etc., ad nauseam*.

2 *Recognising Fascists and Facism*

1 The same is true of accusations based on patently fatuous arguments. One example is the accusation made by Iorwerth Peate in a letter to Gwynfor Evans in 1943, that Plaid Cymru was a Fascist party because

its leaders lacked a 'sense of humour' (Papurau Gwynfor Evans Papers G1/2, National Library of Wales, 17 February 1943). Peate exemplifies the intellectual confusion of so many of the attacks on Plaid Cymru. A former member – he had been one of the two responsible for nominating Saunders Lewis for the party presidency in 1926 following the resignation of Lewis Valentine – Peate was subsequently to quit the party, primarily, it would appear, because he disagreed with the party's readiness to seek support among non-Welsh speakers by publishing party literature in English. Peate believed that the party should operate through the medium of Welsh only (see his letter to Gwynfor Evans, Papurau Gwynfor Evans Papers G1/2, 8 February 1943). Needless to say, he was a prominent supporter of W. J. Gruffydd in the University of Wales by-election.

2   A revealing discussion of attitudes in Britain towards Mussolini may be found in Richard Lamb, *Mussolini and the British* (London: John Murray, 1997). The book cover carries a further quote by Churchill about Mussolini, dating from 1933: 'The Roman genius . . . the greatest lawgiver amongst living men.'

3   Lloyd George is here referring to his visit to meet Hitler the previous year. A virtual gallery containing striking images of the visit can be viewed at *http://www.llgc.org.uk/ardd/dlgeorge/dlg0068.htm*. See also the *apologia* offered up in Emrys Pride, *Why Lloyd George met Hitler* (Risca: The Starling Press, 1981).

4   See Benny Morris, *The Roots of Appeasement: The British Weekly Press and Nazi Germany during the 1930s* (London: Frank Cass, 1991), p. 2.

5   Morris, *The Roots of Appeasement*, p. 47.

6   The failure to admit this basic fact concerning the political culture of the period is one of the most unfortunate characteristics of the various discussions of Saunders Lewis's alleged links to Fascism. See, for example, T. Robin Chapman, *Un Bywyd o Blith Nifer: Cofiant Saunders Lewis* (Llandysul: Gomer, 2006), pp. 147–9.

7   For a revealing discussion of the mutual admiration and cross-fertilisation that characterised the various efforts in Germany, Italy and the United States to escape the claws of the Great Depression see Wolfgang Schivelbusch, *Three New Deals: Reflections on Roosevelt's America, Mussolini's Italy, and Hitler's Germany, 1933–1939* (New York: Picador, 2006).

8   The Fascist parties associated with Mussolini's party are listed in Hans Fredrik Dahl, *Quisling: A Study in Treachery*, trans. Anne-Marie Stanton-Ife (Cambridge: Cambridge University Press), p. 111.

9   The attention given to such extremely marginal parties is referred to in Robert O. Paxton, *The Anatomy of Fascism* (London: Penguin, 2004),

p. 55. A specific discussion of the Icelandic case can be found in Asgeir Gudmundsson, 'Iceland', in Stein U. Larsen, Bernt Hagtvet and Jan Petter Myklebust (eds), *Who were the Fascists?: Social Roots of European Fascism* (Bergen: Universitetsforlaget, 1980), pp. 743–51.

10 Despite the title, Richard Griffiths's contribution is not an exception; see Richard Griffiths, 'Another Form of Fascism: The Cultural Impact of the French "Radical Right" in Britain', in Julie V. Gottleib and Thomas P. Linehan (eds), *The Culture of Fascism: Visions of the Far Right in Britain* (London: I.B. Tauris, 2004), pp. 162–81. Griffiths discusses the influence of the Catholic Radical Right in France on Saunders Lewis and Ambrose Bebb (pp. 173–81), relying heavily on earlier analyses by Gareth Miles and Dafydd Glyn Jones. The author doesn't equate this influence with Fascism, and neither does he suggest that Lewis, Bebb, or the Welsh Nationalist Party more generally speaking, were Fascists.

11 See Wm. Ambrose Bebb, 'Trydydd Anffawd Fawr Cymru' (The Third Great Disaster for Wales), *Y Llenor*, Summer 1924, 109. Bebb makes reference to Primo de Rivera as well as to Lenin and Mussolini. The Primo de Rivera in question was Spain's military dictator between 1923 and 1930; his son was the other Primo de Rivera who founded the Falange.

12 Unfortunately there has been no adequate study of the activities of Oswald Mosley's British Union of Fascists in Wales, beyond Stephen M. Cullen, 'Another Nationalism: The British Union of Fascists in Glamorgan, 1932–40', *Welsh History Review*, 17 (1) (1994), 101–14.

13 *Western Mail and South Wales News*, 1 March 1934. An essay by Catherine Huws published in the November 1933 issue of the *Welsh Nationalist* titled 'Nationalism vs Fascism' discussed BUF activities in south Wales. The thrust of this essay was that every Welsh nationalist should 'fight Fascism as he would a mortal enemy' (9).

14 [Saunders Lewis], 'Nodiadau'r Mis: Ffasgiaeth a Chymru' (Monthly Notes: Fascism and Wales), *Y Ddraig Goch*, July 1934, 6. The quotations in the paragraph that follows are all drawn from this source. Lewis's 'Notes and Comments' column in the June 1934 issue of the *Welsh Nationalist* had already issued the following warning: 'Welsh people will not willingly abandon their cherished freedom of speech nor their freedom of trade union organisation for German or Italian alternatives . . . It is not sufficient to laugh at the Mosleyites – We must see that they are crushed in Wales' (6). In the July issue of the *Welsh Nationalist*, an essay titled 'English Blackshirts and Wales' ends with the following words: 'It belongs to us to rouse the Welsh nation to defend itself from the slave-State of Fascist Ceasarianism or the equally tyrannical bureaucratic State of the Commintern [*sic*]' (5).

15 J. E. Daniel, 'Cenedlaetholdeb Economaidd: Polisi Amaethyddol yr Almaen Heddiw' (Economic Nationalism: Germany's Agricultural Policy Today), *Y Ddraig Goch*, March 1935, 5.

16 [Anon., but Ambrose Bebb], 'Mussolini', *Y Ddraig Goch*, August 1935, 5, 8.

17 As an example, see his interest in cooperative enterprises [*sic*] in Fascist Italy, in Saunders Lewis, *The Case for a Welsh National Development Council* (Caernarfon: Swyddfa'r Blaid Genedlaethol, n.d.), p. 6.

18 For a general introduction, see Stanley G. Payne, *A History of Fascism 1914–45* (London: UCL Press, 1995), pp. 297–302, 400–2, 424–6.

19 [Anon., but Saunders Lewis], 'Notes and Comments', *Welsh Nationalist*, October 1936, 7.

20 Lewis made some positive comments about the Portuguese dictator, Salazar. See 'Notes and Comments' in the *Welsh Nationalist*, September 1936 and October 1936. Salazar's regime may have been extremely unpleasant, but it was not Fascist (Salazar crushed the Fascist movement in his country, perceiving it as a threat). The basis of Lewis's praise for Salazar was the latter's policy of non-intervention with regards the Spanish Civil War, and that the fact that he (like De Valera) was *different* to Mussolini and Hitler. Once more, therefore, what counted in his favour was his perceived distance from Fascism. In a further reference to Salazar in the *Welsh Nationalist* (October 1938), Lewis lauded the dictator alongside De Valera and the notably progressive Labour prime minister in New Zealand, P. J. Savage, as among his 'favourite statesmen'. An eclectic trio, to be sure, but not a trio of political heroes that we might expect a Fascist to embrace.

3 Defining Fascism

1 Among the discussions that I found most illuminating in preparing this book see Robert O. Paxton, *The Anatomy of Fascism* (London; Penguin, 2004), a volume that includes an excellent bibliographical chapter; Stanley G. Payne, *A History of Fascism 1914–45*.

2 Roger Griffin, *The Nature of Fascism* (London: Routledge, 1993), p. 26.

3 Michael Mann, *Fascists* (Cambridge: Cambridge University Press, 2004), p. 13.

4 Mann, *Fascists*, t. 16.

5 Payne, *A History of Fascism 1914–45*, pp. 3–19, esp. p. 7.

6 Payne, *A History of Fascism 1914–45*, p. 16.

7 Payne, *A History of Fascism 1914–45*, p. 16.

8 Paxton, *The Anatomy of Fascism*. It should be noted that Paxton's definition of Fascism is close to that of Michael Mann's. Paxton views Fascism as a form of mass militarised nationalism, which uses violence in pursuit of (internal) purity and of (external) expansion, in order to revive a populace that has been crushed and oppressed; see *The Anatomy of Fascism*, p. 218.

9 Paxton, *The Anatomy of Fascism*, p. 217.

10 Terry Eagleton, 'Carnival of Unreason', *New Statesman*, 3 April 2004.

11 *Perchentyaeth* translates literally as house ownership. It was the term used by Lewis to describe his own economic ideas which stressed the need for a society based on small-scale capitalism. See Wyn Jones, *Rhoi Cymru'n Gyntaf*, pp. 91–5.

12 Saunders Lewis, 'Y Teulu' (The Family), *Canlyn Arthur: Ysgrifau Gwleid-yddol* (Aberystwyth: Gwasg Aberystwyth, 1938), pp. 43–50.

13 In this regard, there is a striking similarity between the attitude of, and even the language used by, Lewis and those US Republican politicians – Herbert Hoover and those of his ilk – who opposed the New Deal. For a sense of the rhetoric used by Conservative opponents to the New Deal more generally, see Schivelbusch, *Three New Deals*.

14 J. E. Daniel, *The Party for Wales*, pp. 14–15.

15 Note in this context the efforts by Aneurin Bevan in 1933 to form a working-class militia in Tredegar, the Workers Freedom Group. See John Campbell, *Nye Bevan and the Mirage of British Socialism* (London: Weidenfeld and Nicolson, 1987), pp. 58–9.

16 Payne, *A History of Fascism 1914–45*, p. 14.

17 Paxton, *The Anatomy of Fascism*, p. 17.

18 Theodor Adorno, 'Freudian Theory and the Pattern of Fascist Propaganda', in *The Culture Industry: Select Essays on Mass Culture* (London: Routledge, 1991), p. 122.

19 Wyn Jones, *Rhoi Cymru'n Gyntaf*, vol. 1, pp. 58–66.

20 These concerns will be further discussed in Richard Wyn Jones, *Syniadaeth Plaid Cymru*, vol. 2 (Caerdydd: Gwasg Prifysgol Cymru, forthcoming).

21 J. E. Daniel, *The Party for Wales*, p. 16.

22 Paxton, *The Anatomy of Fascism*, p. 9.

23 Paxton, *The Anatomy of Fascism*, p. 253, note 31. This is not to suggest that one in every three was a Fascist by conviction; there was a host of other reasons why Italians joined the party. The point is rather that there was no impediment to them joining, which was not the case with Hitler's NSDAP or (after 1934) Oswald Mosley's British Union of Fascists.

24 To emphasise this point further, there were Jews in 1930s Palestine who can be considered to be Fascists. See Joseph Heller, 'The Failure of

Fascism in Jewish Palestine, 1925–1948', in Stein Ugelvik Larsen (ed.), *Fascism outside Europe: The European Impulse against Domestic Conditions in the Diffusion of Global Fascism* (New York: Columbia University Press, 2002), pp. 362–92.

[25] D. Tecwyn Lloyd, *John Saunders Lewis: Y Gyfrol Gyntaf* (Dinbych: Gwasg Gee, 1988), esp. pp. 261–4. See also the following responses: Bruce Grifffiths, 'Cloriannu Albatros Anhepgor', *Barn*, 314 (March 1989), 37–40; Dafydd Elis Thomas, 'Y Deryn Diarth', *Golwg*, 8 December 1988, 22; Dafydd Elis Thomas, 'Freud Cymru', *Radical Wales*, 1 (Winter 1983), 18; Ned Thomas, 'Sandy', *Planet: The Welsh Internationalist*, 72 (December/January 1988/89), 109–10; Dafydd Glyn Jones, 'Dwy Olwg ar Saunders Lewis', *Taliesin*, 66 (March 1989), 16–26; Roy Lewis, 'Saunders Lewis a'r Iddewon', *Y Faner*, 2 December 1988; Meredydd Evans, 'Gwrth-Semitiaeth Saunders Lewis', *Taliesin*, 68 (November 1989), 33–45. For a more recent response, see also Grahame Davies, *Sefyll yn y Bwlch: R. S. Thomas, Saunders Lewis, T. S. Eliot a Simone Weil* (Caerdydd: Gwasg Prifysgol Cymru, 1999), esp. pp. 67–9.

[26] See R. Geraint Gruffydd (ed.), 'Y Dilyw 1939', *Cerddi Saunders Lewis* (Caerdydd: Gwasg Prifysgol Cymru, 1992), pp. 10–12. The poem was first published in 1942. As far as Lewis's other creative work is concerned, some have argued that one of the descriptions in the poem 'Golygfa mewn Caffe' (Café Scene) – referring to 'Blonesgau Whitechapel, Ethiopiaid Golder's Green' (The bloated ladies of Whitechapel, the Ethiopians of Golder's Green) – is anti-Semitic; for example, Davies, *Sefyll yn y Bwlch*, p. 68. In this instance, I am not convinced. On my reading of the poem, Lewis considers Jewish evacuees from London to be one among many outside influences that threaten Welsh culture. He seems to attribute no specific negative characteristics to Jews.

[27] Saunders Lewis, 'Nodiadau'r Mis', *Y Ddraig Goch*, December 1926, 2. In the same essay, Lewis claimed that Lenin was also a Jew.

[28] Lewis, 'Nodiadau'r Mis', Rhagfyr 1926, 2.

[29] Saunders Lewis, 'Nodiadau'r Mis', *Y Ddraig Goch*, June 1933, 2.

[30] Saunders Lewis, 'Nodiadau'r Mis', *Y Ddraig Goch*, August 1934, 2. The Wartski clothes shop was a fixture on Bangor High Street for many decades. It was founded by a Jewish immigrant who had fled to north Wales in the mid nineteenth century to escape Russian pogroms. The Llandudno Wartki's – a jewellers – was also a major shopping destination on the north Wales coast. Polykoff's was another major high street presence in the north west of the country.

[31] See Dafydd Jenkins, *Tân yn Llŷn* (Aberystwyth: Gwasg Aberystwyth, 1937), p. 36.

[32] D. Tecwyn Lloyd, *John Saunders Lewis: Y Gyfrol Gyntaf*, esp. p. 262. With reference to Lewis, Dafydd Elis Thomas states that 'His dealings with Berlin [*ymwneud â Berlin*] and anti-Semitism are also an embarrassment'; Elis Thomas, 'Y Deryn Diarth', 22. This is a truly remarkable comment. As Meredydd Evans notes, 'Not even S.L.'s most vitriolic and blinkered opponents amidst the fervour of war could have used a more open-ended phrase than "dealings with Berlin"'; Meredydd Evans, 'Gwrth-Semitiaeth Saunders Lewis', *Taliesin*, 68 (November 1989), 35.

[33] 'To our knowledge, there is no anti-Semitism in any Welsh writings before the works referred to [by Saunders Lewis] . . .; indeed, it might be said that very few in Welsh-speaking Wales had any knowledge of Jews after the time of the New Testament, at least not until, say, 1967 and the beginning of conflict between Arabs and Jews in the Middle East.' D. Tecwyn Lloyd, *John Saunders Lewis: Y Gyfrol Gyntaf*, pp. 263–4. Others may decide what combination of ignorance, naivety and deliberate attempt at character assassination underpin this observation. I shall simply note two relevant facts in response: (1) anti-Semitic references are not uncommon in medieval Welsh poetry, in *plygain* carols, and so on; and (2) history has repeatedly demonstrated that there is no relationship between knowledge and familiarity on the one hand, and prejudice and racism on the other. As a student in Austria, I witnessed at first hand the extent to which anti-Semitism continues to flourish in that country despite the fact that its Jewish population was decimated during the Second World War. For those unfamiliar with the book, it should perhaps be noted that the central trope in Lloyd's biography is that Lewis was an outsider whose upbringing among the Welsh diaspora on Merseyside (never has Wallasey appeared so distant and exotic) meant that he never truly understood – or was accepted by – Wales and its *gwerin*.

[34] Winston S. Churchill, 'Zionism versus Bolshevism', *The Illustrated Sunday Herald*, 8 February 1920. In fairness, it should also be noted that Churchill sought to use his influence on the White Armies during the Russian civil war to halt the anti-Jewish pogroms that were being perpetrated by their forces. As in the case of Saunders Lewis, there is plenty of evidence to be weighed on the other side of the scales in assessing Churchill's attitude towards Jews.

[35] George Orwell, 'AntiSemitism in Britain' (1945); reprinted in Sonia Orwell and Ian Angus (eds), *The Collected Essays, Journalism and Letters of George Orwell: Volume 3: As I Please 1943–45* (Harmondsworth: Penguin, 1970), p. 385.

[36] *Down and Out in Paris and London* (Harmondsworth: Penguin/Secker & Warburg, 1940) is the most obviously anti-Semitic of Orwell's works.

Even Christopher Hitchens, an enthusiastic admirer of Orwell, recognised his hero's anti-Semitic tendencies; see, for example, Christopher Hitchens, *Why Orwell Matters* (New York: Basic Books, 2003), pp. 9, 101. See also John Newinger, 'Orwell, anti-Semitism and the Holocaust', in John Rodden (ed.), *The Cambridge Companion to George Orwell* (Cambridge: Cambridge University Press, 2007), pp. 112–26. See D. J. Taylor, *Orwell: The Life* (London: Chatto, 2003), pp. 325–6, for evidence of Orwell's beliefs regarding Jewish control of the press.

[37] One example is Lloyd George's famous comment about his fellow Liberal politician Herbert Samuel in 1914: 'a greedy, ambitious and grasping Jew with all the worst characteristics of his race.' Quoted in Jonathan Schneer, *The Balfour Declaration: The Origins of the Arab–Israeli Conflict* (London: Bloomsbury, 2010), p. 126.

[38] W. J. Gruffydd, 'Nodiadau'r Golygydd' (Editorial Notes), *Y Llenor* (Spring 1941), 3.

[39] Saunders Lewis, 'Nodiadau'r Mis' (Monthly Notes), *Y Ddraig Goch*, December 1926, 2.

[40] Saunders Lewis, 'Nodiadau'r Mis' (Monthly Notes), *Y Ddraig Goch*, June 1933, 2.

[41] *Baner ac Amserau Cymru*, 21 April 1938. Quoted in Evans, 'Gwrth-Semitiaeth Saunders Lewis', 44.

[42] For the avoidance of doubt, I should note that my use of the adjective 'casual' is not in any way to trivialise or excuse such prejudice. It is rather an attempt to convey the fact that prejudices of this kind were so deeply sedimented in the culture of the time as to pass almost unnoticed.

[43] Extensive quotes are reproduced in Randall L. Bytwerk, *Julius Streicher: Nazi Editor of the Notorious Anti-Semitic Newspaper 'Der Stürmer'* (New York: Cooper Square, 2001)

[44] Apart from the examples already referred to in this essay, the only other examples which I have been able to identify of what can be considered anti-Jewish prejudice are three separate essays published in the *Welsh Nationalist*: the essay by J. Alun Pugh in the July 1932 issue ('The Anglo-Welshman is always running after English politicians, English Jews or English Trade Union leaders'); the essay by Catherine Huws in the February 1937 issue, which complains that the case of the Penyberth defendants was moved to London, where it would be tried by a jury including 'Englishmen, Irishmen and Jews' who would be quite ignorant of Wales (if this is ethnic prejudice, then it is the only example that I have come across in Plaid Cymru literature of anti-Irish prejudice); and the essay published in the May 1937 issue, again

complaining that the jury at the trial of the Penyberth three would be made up of 'Cockneys and London Jews'.

[45] The same point could also be made in relation to Saunders Lewis, of course. After all, anti-Semitism is an element in the works of Maurice Barrès and Paul Claudel, both of whom influenced some of Lewis's ideas. But is there not a danger that we are – once again – indulging in double standards? After all, we do not expect all of those who admit to having been influenced by the *Communist Manifesto* immediately to disassociate themselves from the crude ethnic prejudices to be found elsewhere in its authors' works. The question of Karl Marx's anti-Semitism has been hotly debated for decades, with much of the discussion distorted by Cold War concerns and motivations. There is no question at all, however, that Marx's co-author and financial backer, Friedrich Engels, harboured a particularly derisive attitude towards the members of 'unhistorical nations', especially towards Slavs. Yet the attitudes of both men towards marginalised peoples was characterised by far more than prejudice alone. For an impressive and balanced scholarly discussion, see Kevin B. Anderson, *Marx at the Margins: On Nationalism, Ethnicity, and Non-Western Societies* (Chicago: The University of Chicago Press, 2010).

4 *Wales During a Decade of War*

[1] Millions more would die before the fighting ended in China in late 1949, when what was left of Chiang's forces fled the mainland to Taiwan.

[2] To avoid taxing the patience of the reader, no detailed discussion of Plaid Cymru's position on Italy's attack on Abyssinia has been included here. That response was characterised by an emphasis on the need to avoid war, and on the rank hypocrisy of England – the imperial power in Kenya, Sudan, etc. – in opposing Italian imperialism in a nearby country.

[3] Robert Stradling, *Wales and the Spanish Civil War: The Dragon's Dearest Cause?* (Cardiff: University of Wales Press, 2004).

[4] For a useful outline of the Roman Catholic Church's political role in Spain between 1918 and 1965, see Mary Vincent, 'Spain', in Tom Buchanan and Martin Conway (eds), *Political Catholicism in Europe, 1918–1965* (Oxford: Clarendon, 1996), pp. 97–128.

[5] Paxton sums up this view in *The Anatomy of Fascism*, pp. 148–50.

[6] The clearest and most authoritative expression of this interpretation is given in the classic work by Hywel Francis, *Miners Against Fascism:*

Wales and the Spanish Civil War (London: Lawrence and Wishart, 1984). For a more popular version, see the bilingual volume by Phil Cope, *Breuddwydwyr Doeth a Ffôl/Wise and Foolish Dreamers* (Caerdydd: Canolfan Materion Rhyngwladol Cymru, 2007).

7   This was also among the most important of Ernest Renan's insights in his discussion of the foundation myths of different nationalisms. See Ernest Renan, 'What is a Nation?', trans. Martin Thom, in Geoff Eley and Ronald Grigor Suny (eds), *Becoming National: A Reader* (New York: Oxford University Press, 1996), p. 45. My point is that the same process of selective memory is also evident in the Labour movement's historiography – and in every other 'productive' historiography for that matter.

8   An authoritative introduction based on the most recent historiographical research is provided in Julián Casanova, *The Spanish Republic and Civil War*, trans. Martin Douch (Cambridge: Cambridge University Press, 2010).

9   In the words of Thomas Charles Edwards in the January 1937 issue of the *Welsh Nationalist*, 'Whatever else is today at stake in Spain, it is not the cause of parliamentary democracy.' The historian Mark Mazower has demonstrated how the vast majority of politicians and populations in Western Europe would have to experience for themselves the horror of the Second World War before they could finally be convinced of the value of democracy; see Mark Mazower, *Dark Continent: Europe's Twentieth Century* (New York: Vintage, 1998). Mazower's argument is as relevant to Wales as it is to Wales's neighbours in other parts of Europe.

10 Another of those who sympathised with Franco's forces was Thomas Jones (T.J.), and to this extent he disagreed with his friend Lloyd George. But it is worth noting that the latter's support for the Republic was a matter of realpolitik and not principle: 'Lloyd George was surprised to discover that although T.J. hoped neither side would win outright victory in the Spanish Civil War, on the whole he favoured Franco. L.G. said a victory for Franco could endanger the whole British position in the Mediterranean.' Ellis, *T.J.: A Life of Dr Thomas Jones*, pp. 406–7.

11 Stradling, *Wales and the Spanish Civil War*, pp. 93–4.

12 Ted Parry, *The Pathologies of Centralism: The Labour Party in Wales to 1957* (unpublished Ph.D. dissertation: Aberystwyth University, 2005), pp. 182–246.

13 Perry Anderson sums up the fate of internationalism in the wake of Stalin's assumption of power in the Communist Party of the Soviet Union in the following terms: 'In short order the activities of the Third International were utterly subordinated to the interests of the Soviet State, as Stalin interpreted them. The upshot was the arresting phenomenon, without equivalent before or since, of an internationalism equally deep and deformed, at once rejecting any loyalty to its own country

and displaying limitless loyalty to another state. Its epic was played out by the International Brigades of the Spanish Civil War . . . With its mixture of heroism and cynicism, selfless solidarity and murderous terror, this was an internationalism perfected and perverted as never before.' Perry Anderson, 'Internationalism: A Breviary', *New Left Review*, II/14 (March/April 2002), p. 15.

[14] Concentrating only on Plaid Cymru's publications in Welsh: Saunders Lewis briefly discussed the situation in Catalonia in the May 1931 issue of *Y Ddraig Goch*. D. J. Davies returned to the same topic in the May 1937 issue, in a short and sympathetic essay. The December 1935 issue included an essay by Cyril P. Cule discussing 'Adfywiad Cenedlaethol Gwlad y Basg' (National Revival in the Basque Country). Cule was one of the most prominent 'internal' critics of Plaid Cymru's position regarding the Spanish Civil War. See the exchanges between him and J. E. Daniel in the November 1936 issue of *Y Ddraig Goch*.

[15] The following observation by Grahame Davies is particularly suggestive: 'Materialism was always Saunders Lewis's main enemy, and communism, which combined atheism with the power of reason and religious faith, was in this regard a more dangerous enemy than fascism, which was simply naked barbarism'; Grahame Davies, *Sefyll yn y Bwlch*, t. 66.

[16] Stradling, *Wales and the Spanish Civil War*, p. 87.

[17] In the paragraphs that follow, I have relied heavily on material collated by Robin Gwyn, *Cwrs y Byd: Dylanwad Athroniaeth Wleidyddol Saunders Lewis ar ei ysgrifau newyddiadurol, 1939–1950* (unpublished M.Phil. dissertation: University of Wales, Bangor, 1991).

[18] 'Nodiadau'r Mis' (Monthly Notes), *Y Ddraig Goch*, November 1938, 8.

[19] 'Nodiadau'r Mis' (Monthly Notes), *Y Ddraig Goch*, January 1940, 4.

[20] It was not only the state that was hypocritical. A number of British Communists sought to justify Stalin's aggression against Finland; among them Raymond Williams who would later become a member of Plaid Cymru, and a considerable influence on some of the party's leading lights. Among his very first publications was a pamphlet co-written with Eric Hobsbawm supporting the Soviet Union's actions. See Fred Inglis, *Raymond Williams* (London: Routledge, 1995), p. 78.

[21] D. Hywel Davies, *The Welsh Nationalist Party 1925–45: A Call to Nationhood*, pp. 229–30.

[22] Robin Gwyn notes that 'one of Saunders Lewis's great heroes during the war years was Gandhi . . . whose attitude to the Second World War was a model for other neutral countries, as well as for Wales.' Gwyn, *Cwrs y Byd*, p. 117.

5 Welsh Political Culture

[1] See H. N. Fieldhouse, 'Correspondence', *International Journal*, 8 (1952–3), 149.

[2] As a further example we might mention the criticism that Welsh nationalists received as a consequence of their efforts to aid Breton nationalists as they faced reprisals from the French state immediately after the Second World War. This is an interesting, dramatic and complicated history, but the key point for the present discussion is that the supporters of Plaid Cymru weren't the only ones to attempt to assist the Bretons. Rather the Welsh establishment *en masse* – with the National Eisteddfod playing a central, mobilising role – endeavoured to ensure that the Bretons received fair treatment. In short, in the case of those Bretons who were accused (some rightly, some wrongly) of Nazi collaboration, supporters of Saunders Lewis and W. J. Gruffydd stood shoulder to shoulder.

[3] For a discussion of the New Party, see Robert Skidelsky, *Oswald Mosley* (London: Macmillan, 1975), pp. 247–82.

[4] Jeffery Hamm's autobiography, titled *Action Replay*, can be downloaded from the website of what remains of Mosley's followers, *www. oswaldmosley.com*. The volume describes Hamm's attempts towards the end of his life to learn Welsh in the company of the London Welsh at Gray's Inn Road (p. 121).

[5] With the only real exception already referred to: Cullen, 'Another Nationalism: The British Union of Fascists in Glamorgan, 1932–40'. Even in this case, however, the broader pattern repeats itself. Two of the essays's fourteen pages are devoted to a discussion of Plaid Cymru, even though Cullen acknowledges that it was not a Fascist party (see pp. 103–4). In addition, an interview with Hamm (by the historian Chris Williams) was published in *Planet* in 1989 (see Jeffrey Hamm, 'The Making of a Welsh Fascist: An interview with Oswald Mosley's former Secretary', *Planet: The Welsh Internationalist*, 74 (April/May 1989), 3–10). The published form of the interview concentrates on Hamm's marginal role in the BUF rather than in his central, leadership role in the post-war Union Movement. On the latter, see inter alia the remarkable Trevor Grundy, *Memoir of a Fascist Childhood: A Boy in Mosley's Britain* (London: Heinemann, 1988). In the *Planet* interview, Hamm was asked about his views on Plaid Cymru. He claims to have been 'ignorant' of the party in the 1930s, but to have 'exchanged letter' with 'Professor [sic] Saunders Lewis' at some point in the 1950s (I cite from the original transcript of the interview). There is, however, no record of such correspondence in the detailed 47-page catalogue of Hamm's papers held at the University

of Birmingham. I am grateful to Chris Williams for his willingness to share memories and materials from the interview.

6 For example, the (deservedly) respected historian Neil Evans has recently suggested that to link the strong showing for Sellick Davies – 'a well-known Liberal . . . [who] seems to have enjoyed Conservative support' – to Fascism is an inflammatory act. This is because, in his view, the New Party was not a clearly Fascist party at the time of the 1931 general election; Neil Evans, 'Politics, Protest and the Public Sphere in Twentieth-Century Wales', *Welsh History Review*, 23 (4), 111. This would be an easier argument to accept if it did not appear that Davies (according to Cullen's evidence) became an active member of the BUF following the demise of the New Party. Indeed, in a generally dismal showing in the 1937 local elections, the Fascists achieved one of their best results outside London in Merthyr; a fact that suggests there was at least a small core in the town that remained faithful to Mosley (Cullen, 'Another Nationalism: The British Union of Fascists in Glamorgan, 1932–40', pp. 106, 112). The same disbelief that Sellick Davies could ever have been a Fascist – 'was poor Sellick Davies ever a Fascist?' – is registered in Robert Griffiths's review of *Miners Against Fascism* in *Radical Wales*, 3 (Summer 1984), 24.

7 Wyn Jones, *Rhoi Cymru'n Gyntaf*, vol. 1, pp. 84–6.

8 Frustration at Plaid Cymru's political naivety has been a common response among those who have joined its ranks after previously being members of other political parties. See, for example, the autobiographical discussion in Phil Williams, *Voice from the Valleys* (Aberystwyth: Plaid Cymru, 1981), pp. 61–77.

9 There are some exceptions, with the occasional academic venturing to discuss what are known in political science as 'one party dominant systems' or, more popularly, 'one-partyism'. See Ian McAllistair, 'The Labour Party in Wales: The Dynamics of One-Partyism', *Llafur*, 3 (1980), 128–39; Richard Wyn Jones and Roger Scully, 'The End of One-Partyism? Party Politics in Wales in the Second Decade of Devolution', *Contemporary Wales*, 21 (2008), 207–17.

10 Richard Wyn Jones and Roger Scully, 'Y Wlad Anghyfrannol' (The Unproportional Country), *Barn*, July/August 2005, 9–11.

11 An extended discussion of the manner in which one-partyism has dictated the politics of devolution is given in Richard Wyn Jones and Roger Scully, *Wales says Yes*, esp. chapters 2 and 4.

12 Lewis continues to claim a central place in the understanding of Welsh nationalism among Plaid Cymru's opponents. I shall note only two very recent examples. First, former First Minister Rhodri Morgan's reference in the *Western Mail* (18 July 2012) to Gruffydd's victory over

Lewis at the University of Wales by-election as one of the most important events in the history of Wales since 1939. He made no mention at all of Gwynfor Evans's victory in Carmarthen in 1966. Morgan's father, T. J. Morgan, was Gruffydd's electoral agent, and one gets the distinct impression that the son sees himself as reliving his father's battles against Plaid Cymru and the man who was the party's president before the outbreak of the Second World War. Second, in an essay to mark the launch of 'Gorwel' – a Welsh centre-right think-tank – by the Conservative Assembly Member David Melding in July 2012, Tim Williams (a prominent member of the No Campaign in 1997) managed to devote the greater part of his discussion to an attack on Saunders Lewis ('fingered as a fascist from early on by his peers') and Lewis's supposed admiration for Hitler and Mussolini, his anti-Semitism, and the usual, wearily familiar claims: 'Lewis was a fellow traveller of the Axis powers and so was his Party under his leadership.' (See *http://www.clickonwales. org/2012/07/economic-crisis-1-wales-needs-radical-transformation/* – accessed 24 August 2012.)

[13] Chris Harvie, 'The Folk and the Gwerin: The Myth and Reality of Popular Political Culture in 19th Century Scotland and Wales', *Proceedings of the British Academy*, 80 (1991), 19–48.

[14] For an introduction to Bauer's ideas see Ephraim Nimni, *Marxism and Nationalism: Theoretical Origins of a Political Crisis* (London: Pluto, 1981), pp. 119–84.

[15] Lest this should appear to be a case of stating the obvious, it should be emphasised that contemporary international evidence indicates that Wales is one of the few European 'regions' where 'regional' identity functions as a 'national' identity. Indeed, if we focus only on Western Europe, it is only in Wales, Scotland, Flanders, Catalonia and the Basque Country that it can be confidently stated that the majority harbour a sub-state identity that they would consider to be a *national* identity. See the evidence – including contributions by the present author – collected in Ailsa Henderson, Charlie Jeffery and Dan Wincott (eds), *Citizens after the Nation State: Regional Public Attitudes Beyond Methodological Nationalism* (Basingstoke: Palgrave, 2013).

6 Conclusion: Redemption and Exclusion

[1] Jan Morris, *Our First Leader: A Welsh Fable* (Llandysul: Gomer, 2000); Twm Morys dros Jan Morris, *Ein Llyw Cyntaf* (Llandysul: Gomer, 2001).

Bibliography

Archives

Leo Abse Papers, National Library of Wales.
Gwilym Davies Papers, National Library of Wales.
Thomas Jones Papers, National Library of Wales.
D. Francis Roberts Papers, National Library of Wales.

Newspapers and Journals

Baner ac Amserau Cymru
Cambrian News
Daily Herald
Ddraig Goch, Y
Golwg
Guardian, The
Sun, The
Tribune
Welsh Mirror
Welsh Nationalist

Books and Periodicals

Adorno, Theodor W., 'Freudian Theory and the Pattern of Fascist
Propaganda', *The Culture Industry: Select Essays on Mass Culture*
(London: Routledge, 1991), 132–57.

Anderson, Kevin B., *Marx at the Margins: On Nationalism, Ethnicity, and Non-Western Societies* (Chicago: The University of Chicago Press, 2010).

Anderson, Perry, 'Internationalism: A Breviary', *New Left Review* II/14 (March/April 2002), 5–25.

Bebb, W. Ambrose, '"Cymru Gyfan a'r Blaid Genedlaethol Gymreig": Ateb i'r Parch. Gwilym Davies', *Y Traethodydd*, 426 (January 1943), 1–14.

Bebb, W. Ambrose, *Dydd-lyfr Pythefnos, neu Y Ddawns Angau* (Bangor: Sackville Printing Works, 1939).

Bebb, W. Ambrose, 'Mussolini', *Y Ddraig Goch* (August 1935), 5, 8.

Bebb, W. Ambrose, 'Trydydd Anffawd Fawr Cymru', *Y Llenor* (Summer 1924), 103–9.

Benda, Julien, *La trahison des clercs* (Paris: B. Grasset, 1927).

Brooks, Simon, 'The Idiom of Race: The "Racist Nationalist" in Wales as Bogeyman', in T. Robin Chapman (ed.), *The Idiom of Dissent: Protest and Propaganda in Wales*, Foreword by Dafydd Elis-Thomas (Llandysul: Gomer, 2006), 139–65.

Bytwerk, Randall L., *Julius Streicher: Nazi Editor of the Notorious Anti-Semitic Newspaper 'Der Stürmer'* (New York: Cooper Square, 2001).

Campbell, John, *Nye Bevan and the Mirage of British Socialism* (London: Weidenfeld and Nicolson, 1987).

Casanova, Julián, *The Spanish Republic and Civil War*, trans. Martin Douch (Cambridge: Cambridge University Press, 2010).

Chapman, T. Robin, *W. J. Gruffydd* (Caerdydd: Gwasg Prifysgol Cymru, 1993).

Chapman, T. Robin, *W. Ambrose Bebb* (Caerdydd: Gwasg Prifysgol Cymru, 1997).

Chapman, T. Robin, *Un Bywyd o Blith Nifer: Cofiant Saunders Lewis* (Llandysul: Gomer, 2006).

Churchill, Winston S., 'Zionism versus Bolshevism', *The Illustrated Sunday Herald* (8 February 1920),

Cope, Phil, *Breuddwydwyr Doeth a Ffôl/Wise and Foolish Dreamers* (Cardiff: Welsh Centre for International Affairs, 2007).

Cule, Cyril P., 'Adfywiad Cenedlaethol Gwlad y Basg', *Y Ddraig Goch* (December 1935), 2.

Cullen, Stephen M., 'Another Nationalism: The British Union of Fascists in Glamorgan, 1932–40', *Welsh History Review*, 17/1 (1994), 101–14.

Dahl, Hans Frederik, *Quisling: A Study in Treachery*, trans. Anne-Marie Stanton-Ife (Cambridge: Cambridge University Press, 1999).

Daniel, J. E., 'Cenedlaetholdeb Economaidd: Polisi Amaethyddol yr Almaen Heddiw', *Y Ddraig Goch* (March 1935), 5.

David, Wayne, *Remaining True: A Biography of Ness Edwards*, Foreword by Neil Kinnock (Caerphilly: Caerphilly Local History Society, 2006).

Davies, D. Hywel, *The Welsh Nationalist Party 1925–45: A Call to Nationhood* (Cardiff: University of Wales Press, 1983).

Davies, Gwilym, *Cymru Gyfan a'r Blaid Genedlaethol Gymreig* (Caernarfon: Argraffdy'r Methodistiaid Calfinaidd, 1942).

Davies, Gwilym, 'Cymru Gyfan a'r Blaid Genedlaethol Gymreig', *Y Traethodydd*, 424 (July 1942), 97–111.

Davies, Gwilym, '"Cymru'n Ddwy?" Ateb i Mr. Ambrose Bebb', *Y Traethodydd*, 427 (April 1943), 74–88.

Davies, John, *Broadcasting and the BBC in Wales* (Cardiff: University of Wales Press, 1994).

Ellis, E. L., *T.J.: A Life of Dr Thomas Jones* (Cardiff: University of Wales Press, 1992).

Evans, D. Emrys, 'Y Rhyfel a'r Dewis', *Y Llenor* (Summer 1941), 69–76.

Evans, Gwynfor, *Bywyd Cymro*, ed. Manon Rhys (Caernarfon: Gwasg Gwynedd, 1982).

Evans, Gwynfor, *Diwedd Prydeindod* (Talybont: Y Lolfa, 1981).

Evans, Meredydd, 'Gwrth-Semitiaeth Saunders Lewis', *Taliesin*, 68 (November 1989), 33–45.

Evans, Neil, 'Politics, Protest and the Public Sphere in Twentieth-Century Wales', *Welsh History Review*, 23/4 (2007), 108–12.

Evans, Rhys, *Gwynfor: Rhag Pob Brad* (Talybont: Y Lolfa, 2005).

Fieldhouse H. N., 'Correspondence', *International Journal*, 8 (1952–3), 149.

Francis, Hywel, *Miners Against Fascism: Wales and the Spanish Civil War* (London: Lawrence and Wishart, 1984).

Griffin, Roger, *The Nature of Fascism* (London: Routledge, 1993).

Griffiths, Bruce, 'Cloriannu Albatros Anhepgor', *Barn*, 314 (March 1989), 37–40.

Griffiths, Richard, 'Another Form of Fascism: The Cultural Impact of the French "Radical Right" in Britain', in Julie V. Gottlieb and Thomas P. Linehan (eds), *The Culture of Fascism: Visions of the Far Right in Britain* (London: I.B. Tauris, 2004), 162–81.

Gruffydd, R. Geraint (ed.), *Cerddi Saunders Lewis* (Caerdydd: Gwasg Prifysgol Cymru, 1992).

Gruffydd, W. J., 'Atebiad y Golygydd i Mr. Saunders Lewis', *Y Llenor* (Summer 1927), 78–95.

Gruffydd, W. J., 'Mae'r gwylliaid ar y ffordd', *Y Llenor* (Autumn 1940), 112–26.

Gruffydd, W. J., 'Nodiadau'r Golygydd', *Y Llenor* (Spring 1941), 1–4.

Gruffydd, W. J., 'Nodiadau'r Golygydd', *Y Llenor* (Winter 1940), 161–8.

Gudmundsson, Asgeir, 'Iceland', in Stein U. Larsen, Bernt Hagtvet and Jan Petter Myklebust (eds), *Who were the Fascists?: Social Roots of European Fascism* (Bergen: Universitetsforlaget, 1980), 743–51.

Gwyn, Robin, *Cwrs y Byd: Dylanwad Athroniaeth Wleidyddol Saunders Lewis ar ei ysgrifau newyddiadurol, 1939–1950*, unpublished M.Phil. thesis, Bangor University, 1991.

Hamm, Jeffrey, *Action Replay*. Published at *www.oswaldmosley.com*.

Hamm, Jeffrey, 'The Making of a Welsh Fascist: An interview with Oswald Mosley's former Secretary', *Planet: The Welsh Internationalist*, 74 (April/May 1989), 3–10.

Harvie, Chris, 'The Folk and the Gwerin: The Myth and Reality of Popular Political Culture in 19th Century Scotland and Wales', *Proceedings of the British Academy*, 80 (1991), 19–48.

Heller, Joseph, 'The Failure of Fascism in Jewish Palestine, 1925–1948', in Stein Ugelvik Larsen (ed.), *Fascism outside Europe: The European Impulse against Domestic Conditions in the Diffusion of Global Fascism* (New York: Columbia University Press, 2002), 362–92.

Henderson, Ailsa, Charlie Jeffery and Dan Wincott (eds), *Citizens after the Nation State: Regional Public Attitudes Beyond Methological Nationalism* (Palgrave, forthcoming).

Hincks, Rhisiart, *E. Prosser Rhys 1901–45* (Llandysul: Gomer, 1980).

Hitchens, Christopher, *Why Orwell Matters* (New York: Basic Books, 2003).

Hughes, Trystan Owain, *Winds of Change: The Roman Catholic Church and Society in Wales, 1916–92* (Cardiff: University of Wales Press, 1999).

Inglis, Fred, *Raymond Williams* (London: Routledge, 1995).

Jarman, A. O. H., 'Y Blaid a'r Ail Ryfel Byd', in John Davies (ed.), *Cymru'n Deffro: Hanes y Blaid Genedlaethol* (Talybont: Y Lolfa, 1981), 67–92.

Jenkins, Dafydd, *Tân yn Llŷn* (Aberystwyth: Gwasg Aberystwyth, 1937).

Jones, Dafydd Glyn, 'Dwy Olwg ar Saunders Lewis', *Taliesin*, 66 (March 1989), 16–26.

Jones, E. D. and Brynley F. Roberts (eds), *Y Bywgraffiadur Cymreig 1951–1970* (Llundain: Anrhydeddus Gymdeithas y Cymmrodorion, 1997).

Jones, J. Graham, 'The Parliament for Wales Campaign 1950–1956', *Welsh History Review*, 16/2 (1992), 207–36.

Jones, Tegwyn, 'Etholiad y Brifysgol 1943', *Y Faner* (2, 9, 16, 23 Medi 1977).

Jones, T. J., *The Native Never Returns* (London: W. Griffiths & Co., 1946).

Kershaw, Ian, *Making Friends with Hitler: Lord Londonderry and Britain's Road to War* (London: Allen Lane, 2004).

Lamb, Richard, *Mussolini and the British* (London: John Murray, 1997).

Lewis, Roy, 'Saunders Lewis a'r Iddewon', *Y Faner* (2 December 1988).

Lewis, Saunders, 'English Blackshirts and Wales', *Welsh Nationalist* (July 1934), 5.

Lewis, Saunders, 'Llythyr ynghylch Catholigiaeth', *Y Llenor* (Summer 1927), 72–7.

Lewis, Saunders, *The Party for Wales*, trans. Emyr Humphreys (Caernarfon: Plaid Genedlaethol Cymru, n.d.)

Lewis, Saunders, *The Case for a Welsh National Development Council* (Caernarfon: Swyddfa'r Blaid Genedlaethol, n.d.)

Lewis, Saunders, 'Undebau Llafur', *Y Ddraig Goch* (November 1932); reprinted in Saunders Lewis, *Canlyn Arthur: Ysgrifau Gwleidyddol* (Llandysul: Gomer, 1985), 55–60.

Lewis, Saunders and J. E. Daniel, *Plaid Cymru Gyfan: Atebion Saunders Lewis a J. E. Daniel i Mr. [sic] Gwilym Davies* (Caernarfon: Plaid Genedlaethol Cymru, 1942).

Lloyd, D. Tecwyn, *John Saunders Lewis: Y Gyfrol Gyntaf* (Dinbych: Gwasg Gee, 1988).

Mazower, Mark, *Dark Continent: Europe's Twentieth Century* (New York: Vintage, 1998).

McAllistair, Ian, 'The Labour Party in Wales: The Dynamics of One-Partyism', *Llafur*, 3 (1980), 128–39.

McGuinness, Patrick, 'Racism in Welsh Politics', *Planet: The Welsh Internationalist*, 159 (June/July 2003), 7–12.

McGuinness, Patrick, 'Reflections in the "Welsh" Mirror', *Planet: The Welsh Internationalist*, 153 (June/July 2002), 6–12.

McGuinness, Patrick, 'The War on Welsh: An Update', *Planet: The Welsh Internationalist*, 155 (October/November 2002), 59–9.

Miles, Gareth, 'W. Ambrose Bebb', in Derec Llwyd Morgan (ed.), *Adnabod Deg: Portreadau o Ddeg o Arweinwyr Cynnar y Blaid Genedlaethol* (Dinbych: Gwasg Gee, 1977), 77–95.

Morris, Benny, *The Roots of Appeasement: The British Weekly Press and Nazi Germany during the 1930s* (London: Frank Cass, 1991).

Morris, Jan, *Our First Leader: A Welsh Fable* (Llandysul: Gomer, 2000).

Morys, Twm, for Jan Morris, *Ein Llyw Cyntaf* (Llandysul: Gomer, 2001).

Newinger, John, 'Orwell, anti-Semitism and the Holocaust', in John Rodden (ed.), *The Cambridge Companion to George Orwell* (Cambridge: Cambridge University Press, 2007), 112–26.

Nimni, Ephraim, *Marxism and Nationalism: Theoretical Origins of a Political Crisis* (London: Pluto, 1981).

O'Leary, Paul, 'When Was Anti-Catholicism? The Case of Nineteenth- and the Twentieth-Century Wales', *The Journal of Ecclesiastical Studies*, 56/2 (2005), 308–25.

Orwell, George, 'AntiSemitism in Britain', in Sonia Orwell and Ian Angus (eds), *The Collected Essays, Journalism and Letters of George Orwell: Volume 3: As I Please 1943–45* (Harmondsworth: Penguin 1970), 378–88.

Orwell, George, *Down and Out in Paris and London* (Harmondsworth: Penguin/Secker & Warburg, 1940).

Parry, Ted, *The Pathologies of Centralism: The Labour Party in Wales to 1957*, unpublished Ph.D. thesis, Aberystwyth University, 2005.

Patterson, Samuel C. and Anthony Mughan, *Senates: Bicameralism in the Contemporary World* (Columbus: Ohio State, 1999).

Paxton, Robert O., *The Anatomy of Fascism* (London: Penguin, 2004).

Pride, Emrys, *Why Lloyd George met Hitler* (Risca: The Starling Press, 1981).

Renan, Ernest, 'What is a Nation?', trans. Martin Thom, in Geoff Eley and Ronald Grigor Suny (eds), *Becoming National: A Reader* (New York: Oxford University Press, 1996), 42–56.

Report of the Commission on the Powers and Electoral Arrangements of the National Assembly for Wales, *Report of the Richard Commission* (Cardiff: National Assembly for Wales, 2004).

Rock, William R., *British Appeasement in the 1930s* (London: Edward Elgar, 1977).

Schivelbusch, Wolfgang, *Three New Deals: Reflections on Roosevelt's America, Mussolini's Italy, and Hitler's Germany, 1933–1939* (New York: Picador, 2006).

Schneer, Jonathan, *The Balfour Declaration: The Origins of the Arab–Israeli Conflict* (London: Bloomsbury, 2010).

Skidelsky, Robert, *Oswald Mosley* (London: Macmillan, 1975).

Sternhell, Zeev, *Neither Left nor Right: Fascist Ideology in France*, trans. David Maisel (London: University of California Press, 1986).

Stradling, Robert, *Wales and the Spanish Civil War: The Dragon's Dearest Cause?* (Cardiff: University of Wales Press, 2004).

Taylor, D. J., *Orwell: The Life* (London: Chatto, 2003).

Thomas, Ned, 'Sandy', *Planet: the Welsh Internationalist*, 72 (December/ January 1988/89), 109–10.

Vincent, Mary, 'Spain', in Tom Buchanan and Martin Conway (eds), *Political Catholicism in Europe, 1918–1965* (Oxford: Clarendon, 1996), 97–128.

Waters, Lee, *From Little Acorns . . .: The Fall and Rise of Devolution in the Welsh Labour Party, 1979–1995* (Cardiff: Wales Governance Centre, 2013).

Weber, Eugen, *Action Française: Royalism and Reaction in Twentieth Century France* (Stanford: Stanford University Press, 1962).

Weitz, John, *Hitler's Diplomat: Joachim von Ribbentrop* (London: Phoenix Giant, 1992).

Williams, Phil, *Voice from the Valleys* (Aberystwyth: Plaid Cymru, 1981).

Wyn Jones, Richard, *Rhoi Cymru'n Gyntaf: Syniadaeth Plaid Cymru Cyf. 1* (Caerdydd: Gwasg Prifysgol Cymru, 2007).

Wyn Jones, Richard and Roger Scully, 'The End of One-Partyism? Party Politics in Wales in the Second Decade of Devolution', *Contemporary Wales*, 21 (2008), 207–17.

Wyn Jones, Richard and Roger Scully, *Wales says Yes: Devolution and the 2011 Welsh Referendum* (Cardiff: University of Wales Press, 2012).

Wyn Jones, Richard and Roger Scully, 'Y Wlad Anghyfrannol', *Barn* (July/August 2005), 9–11.

Index

Index

Index

Index